...an writing again and ...to

Reference your to S 12 ... o if the

that one fears contamination ...

Your letter came to me ... Abu Lissan

Dead Sea & I carried it with me down

all that I have had — only a month

marines ... & him it is all over for anoth...

eyes would prevent ... service for you

myself. I have been so violently uproo...

unreal. I have dropped all I can

moment when & where I see them.

Arab rebellion against Turkey, & f...

out of the Arab picture as I can. So

in fancy dress, in a strange language

T. E. Lawrence

THE BRITISH LIBRARY
HISTORIC LIVES

T. E. Lawrence

Malcolm Brown

The British Library

The British Library would like to thank the following for permission to reproduce copyright material and illustrations: The Trustees of the Seven Pillars of Wisdom Trust, the Imperial War Museum, the Bodleian Library, the British Museum and other named copyright holders. While every effort has been made to trace and acknowledge all copyright holders, we would like to apologise for any errors or omissions.

Cover illustration: Lawrence in Arab dress, photographed by Harry Chase, c. 1918.
Courtesy of Lowell Thomas, Jr.

Half-title page illustration: Lawrence, taken from Charlotte Shaw's papers.
The British Library, Add. MS 56499, f.34

Title-page illustration: Lawrence driving through Damascus, 1 October 1918.
Rolls-Royce Heritage Trust

First published in 2003 by
The British Library
96 Euston Road
London NW1 2DB

Text © 2003 Malcolm Brown
Illustrations © 2003 The British Library Board and other named copyright holders

British Library Cataloguing in Publication Data
A catalogue record for this book is available from The British Library

ISBN 0 7123 4809 3

Designed and typeset by
Andrew Barron @ thextension

Printed in Hong Kong by
South Sea International Press

Contents

'... the dreamers of the day are dangerous men, for they may act their dream with open eyes to make it possible. This I did... .'

Introduction: a dreamer of the day

26 August 1907. A nineteen-year-old youth bicycles along a narrow causeway jutting northwards from the coast of northern France. Ahead of him towers that steep pyramid of monastery, rampart and rock known as Mont St Michel. The bicycle is advanced for its time, with dropped handlebars and a three-speed gear. The rider is short, even slight in build, but also muscular, and it would be uncharacteristic if he were not cycling at speed and with a determined, ferocious energy. The head is fractionally large for the body; this, plus the quality of the features – high forehead, firm chin, striking blue eyes – compensate remarkably for any physical disadvantage, giving an overall impression of strength and vigour. The eyes gleam with an alert curiosity and the pleasure of responding to a challenge; and they doubtless shone with a particular enthusiasm that August afternoon, for within hours he was writing in a letter to his family in England:

Here I am at last about to spend a night at the Mont. The dream of years is fulfilled. It is a perfect evening; the tide is high and comes some 20 feet up the street. In addition the stars are out most beautifully, and the moon is, they say, just about to rise. The phosphorescence in the water interests me specially: I have only seen it once or twice before, and never so well as tonight. The whole sea, when oars are dipped into it, seems to blaze, for several feet around...

He had been in France for three weeks, first with his father as companion and then alone. He had visited numerous medieval churches and castles across Normandy and Brittany, sketching, drawing detailed plans, photographing, frequently climbing to dangerous heights on jagged ruins to find unusual and more dramatic viewpoints. At Dinard, where he had lived briefly as a child, and which he reached after a particularly demanding ride from Angers, he had found lodgings with a family known to him, the Chaignons: 'When I spoke and

Previous page: Captain T.E. Lawrence
in his newly acquired Arab clothes, in
early 1917, with the Arab camp at Wejh
behind him.
Imperial War Museum Q 59075

revealed myself there was a most enthusiastic scene: All yelled welcome at once...
M Corbeil was with them, and collapsed when he heard where I had come from.
I have given them a topic of conversation for a week. Deux cent cinquante
kilometres, Ah la-la, qu'il est merveilleux.'

Given the notorious camber of most French roads at the time, it is hardly
surprising that his hosts marvelled at his achievement of bicycling 250 kilometres
in a day – over 150 miles.

The letter was signed, as were all his letters at this time, 'Ned'. Throughout
his youth, to both friends and family he was always 'Ned Lawrence'. It was the
first of a series of names, some real, some invented, which he would adopt during
his short life.

He was again in France in the following year, 1908, undertaking a far more
ambitious journey. Travelling this time entirely alone, he explored a handful of
Norman castles, then headed south – achieving the 500 miles to Avignon in
ten days – until, riding on from Arles, he stopped at a particular viewpoint where
he had 'a most delightful surprise... I was looking from the edge of a precipice
down the valley far over the plain, watching the green changing into brown, and
the brown into a grey line far away over the horizon, when suddenly the sun
leaped from behind a cloud, and a sort of silver shiver passed over the grey:
then I understood, and instinctively burst out with a cry of "Thalassa, Thalassa".'

'The Sea! The Sea!': it was the famous cry of Xenophon's Army of the Ten
Thousand when, on their way back to Greece from Mesopotamia in 401 BC,
they caught their first glimpse of the Black Sea. For Lawrence it did not spoil
the classical allusion, indeed rather enriched it, that the sea he thought he had
sighted was the historic Mediterranean. What he had actually seen were some
lakes just short of the Mediterranean shore, but within hours he was bathing

The cloisters at Mont St Michel, photographed by 'Ned' Lawrence during his 1907 French journey. 'The insides of the buildings on the Mont are lovely,' he wrote in a letter home, though he claimed to have been 'horrified by the exterior'. From *Crusader Castles*, by T.E. Lawrence.
The British Library, C98.i.14

in the sea and revelling in it:
It was as warm as may be pleasant, and the water refreshingly delicious: I felt at last I had reached the way to the South, and all the glorious East; Greece, Carthage, Egypt, Tyre, Syria, Italy, Spain, Sicily, Crete… they were all there, and all within reach… of me. I fancy I know now better than Keats what Cortes felt like, 'silent upon a peak in Darien'. Oh I must get down here, – farther out – again! Really this getting to the sea has almost overturned my mental balance: I would accept a passage for Greece tomorrow….

From later evidence we know that the mind of this 'pocket Hercules' (his own description of twenty years later, written in anger at a journalist who had called him a physical weakling) was teeming with dreams and ambitions way beyond those of a mere would-be traveller to antique lands. In a notable chapter of his most widely read work – strikingly entitled *Seven Pillars of Wisdom* – he would admit to hoping to be a general, and knighted, when thirty. In its final paragraph he would state that

Opposite: Lawrence's own map, showing places visited during his French travels as a young man. The scatter of towns and castles named might seem to suggest he rode at random; in fact, he carefully planned his journeys in advance with the help of a contemporary *Handbook to France* and works on medieval French architecture. From *Crusader Castles*, by T.E. Lawrence. *The British Library, C98.i.14*

he 'had dreamed at the City School in Oxford, of hustling into form, while I lived, the new Asia which time was inexorably bringing upon us'. From letters of the early 1920s to literary friends we know that he also harboured an ambition to write a classic work that would match the masterpieces of such as Melville, Dostoevsky, Tolstoy, Cervantes and Rabelais.

He acknowledged the driving power of his ambitions in a striking passage of *Seven Pillars of Wisdom*: 'All men dream: but not equally. Those who dream by night in the dusty recesses of their minds wake in the day to find that it was vanity; but the dreamers of the day are dangerous men, for they may act their dream with open eyes to make it possible. This I did…'

But if he was, in his own terms, 'a dangerous man', the course he would take would also be fraught with danger. Risk came naturally to him and it was perhaps inevitable that he was not one likely to die peaceably in his bed.

His cry 'Thalassa! Thalassa!', he told his family, 'startled an eagle from the opposite hill [and] two French tourists who came rushing up hoping to find another of the disgusting murders their papers make such a fuss about I suppose', and were then disappointed when they heard it was 'only the Mediterranean'. Such reactions apart, doubtless few noticed and none remembered the mildly eccentric English youth as he rode off at high pace along the French roads; but the time would come when his fame would not allow him to show his face in public without being pursued by sycophants, suitors, would-be disciples or the representatives of the popular press. He would join that small band of British adventurers who are known by the territory in which they spent sometimes their finest and sometimes their final hours: Clive of India, Gordon of Khartoum, Scott of the Antarctic. And he would become the subject of one the most popular and memorable movies ever made.

FRANCE
PLACES VISITED
1907. 1908.

He would also become a figure of continuing controversy; revered by some, reviled by others. Brilliant, bogus, a near genius, an arrogant self-promoting charlatan: the opinions would vary from one extreme to the other. Indeed, there seems little chance of ever arriving at a consensus on the character and achievements of this extraordinary man. Perhaps it is just as well. An unquestioned reputation can very easily turn into a dead one. Figures who rise above all controversy are all too often lost in the clouds. Certainly no such fate awaits the man styled, since the last century's twenties and his own early thirties, as 'Lawrence of Arabia'.

'Farther out' was a key phrase from his strenuous journey of 1908 and a key motive for so much of his life, yet in the end there was an almost pathetic figure creeping miserably into his own private bolt-hole deep in the English countryside, hiding from the world and admitting to feeling like 'a leaf fallen from [a] tree'.

1

Thomas Edward Lawrence was, it can fairly be said, extraordinary from birth. He emerged out of a background that could well have provided the setting for a Victorian novel.

A flawed inheritance

Thomas Edward Lawrence was, it can fairly be said, extraordinary from birth. He emerged out of a background that could well have provided the setting for a Victorian novel. Place the story in nineteenth-century Yorkshire and he could almost have been a son of Charlotte Brontë's best-known heroine, Jane Eyre, and her darkly romantic lover, Edward Rochester. There are distinct similarities of plot. A handsome country landowner finds himself in bewilderment and distress as his once attractive wife becomes increasingly subject to mania, though of an all-possessive religious variety, not the wild madness that affected Bertha Rochester. A young governess of humble origin arrives to look after the family offspring; not one 'natural' child as in the fictional account (the illegitimacy would come later and in abundance), but four legally conceived daughters. Penned together in the isolation of a largely empty countryside, while the lady of the manor pursues a regime of harsh rules and overbearing religious observance, master and governess fall in love. However, no convenient house fire intervenes as in Charlotte Brontë's masterpiece to remove the unwanted wife and thus allow a lawful solution to the lovers' dilemma, so at this point the plots markedly diverge. The memorable pay-off line to Jane Eyre's story 'Reader, I married him' was not, nor would ever be, possible in the case of this particular governess. Caught between the prospect of restraint and respectability on the one hand, and sin and sex on the other, the lovers opted for the latter and with a vengeance. How long it took for the situation to develop, who seduced whom or whether there was some kind of overwhelming attraction between the two is not known. What is undeniable is that once they broke the seventh commandment they never looked back, but went on to produce a family of five fine but illegitimate sons, while themselves maintaining a lifelong devotion and fidelity. The twist in the story is that the young governess was no flighty libertine but was in her way as profoundly religious as the woman she supplanted.

Previous page: No 2 Polstead Road,
Oxford, the Lawrence family home
from 1896. In the new suburb of North
Oxford, where housing ranged from
detached Gothic mansions to
two-storeyed workers' dwellings, the
Lawrences' semi-detached, red-brick
villa was suitably in the middle ground:
neither too pretentious, nor too humble.
Author collection

Below: South Hill, County Westmeath,
Ireland; the country house in the
hinterland of Dublin where Lawrence's
story began but which he never visited.
The house was later purchased by the
Catholic order of the Charity Sisters of
Jesus and Mary.
Little, Brown, Boston Mass

The story's real location was not Yorkshire but Ireland, the house was South Hill, County Westmeath, some twenty miles from Dublin, but the plot has a hint of social class no Brontë would have thought of in that the landowner concerned, Thomas Robert Tighe Chapman, was a product of England's most famous public school, Eton, and the heir to a baronetcy – an inheritance which, thanks to his fall from grace, he would never be free to acknowledge. There was some attempt to conceal the birth of the first child, but their ruse was discovered when the butler of the senior, ancestral Chapman household, at nearby Killua Castle, overheard the governess giving her name as Mrs Chapman in a grocer's shop in Dublin. He followed her to her lodgings, where he discovered that the landowner and his employee were co-habiting as man and wife. The secret once out, Thomas Chapman had the choice of staying loyal to his legal spouse, Edith, or of taking off with the woman he loved but with whom he could live only outside the law. He appears not to have hesitated. The governess had been christened Sarah, was from Scotland and was herself illegitimate. There has long been uncertainty about her surname but it appears that she had at one stage taken to calling herself Lawrence; indeed it is probable that Lawrence was the name of her natural father, the eighteen-year-old son of her mother's employer, possibly using his status to have his way with a woman eleven years his senior. However it came about, the new rootless couple adopted the name as a convenient alias as, like the lovers in Keats's *The Eve of St Agnes*, they fled into the night.

One touching detail softens the otherwise hard image of the abandoned Edith Chapman: when the governess, doubtless fearing the signs of her pregnancy would soon become obvious, relinquished her post, Edith gave her a locket containing the photographs of her four daughters as a keepsake.

Thomas and Sarah – or 'Mr and Mrs T.R. Lawrence' as they now presented themselves to the world – were remarkably slow to settle; instead they became for a number of years wanderers, virtual refugees, with no permanent roof over their heads. Dublin had been the convenient birthplace of their first son, Montagu Robert, known as 'Bob', in 1885. By contrast the birthplaces of the others were so widely separated that it is almost as though they were trying to shake off sleuths on their trail. Thomas Edward, 'Ned', the future Lawrence of Arabia, was born in north Wales in 1888; William George, 'Will', was born in Scotland in 1889; Frank Helier in the Channel Islands in 1893, while their youngest, Arnold Walter, 'Arnie', was born in 1900 in the ancient university city of Oxford, where they at last found an abiding habitation in 1896. Before that

they had also lived in Brittany, the Isle of Wight and the New Forest.

Arrived in Oxford they were able to make a home in a new expanding suburb where many of the university's dons, recently freed from the restraints of their traditional celibacy, were now bringing up burgeoning young families. They acquired one of North Oxford's many newly built houses – red-brick, semi-detached but with three floors and substantial garden; not of the highest class but not of the most modest either – where to all intents and purposes they lived the life of an ordinary, respectful couple, their secret concealed behind the sturdy doors and discreet curtains of 2 Polstead Road.

One significant bonus of moving to Oxford is that they found a church to worship in where they heard a doctrine being expounded that seemed especially benign to a couple living in sin. Just across the road from Oxford's grandest college, Christ Church, stood, as it stands to this day, the modest sanctuary of St Aldates, where the priest in charge was a leading evangelical, Canon A.M.W. Christopher. His belief in the attainability of salvation through good works, no matter how tainted the sinner, encouraged them in the hope that they might win forgiveness through some suitable act or acts of atonement. If, for example, their sons could be offered like so many young Samuels to the service of the Lord, all might be well. Oxford at this time was a city in religious ferment, boasting several foundations devoted to the new Anglican High Church movement, but three times every Sunday the Lawrences walked or bicycled past a number of them to the low-church certainties of a faith that offered the reassurance for which Sarah Lawrence in particular craved. Bob, the eldest son, swiftly discovered the vocation that would eventually turn him into a medical missionary in China. Ned himself was seen in the distinctive pill-box cap of the Church Lads' Brigade and became, for a time, a Sunday School teacher. Will and Frank also cheerfully conformed. At this stage Sarah Lawrence's hopes seemed in fine trim, but it should be noted that as a woman of strong will she might get her way without difficulty at this stage, but she would sow the seeds of discord, even rebellion, in at least two of her sons: her youngest, Arnold, who would ultimately repudiate all she stood for, and T.E. Lawrence himself, who would never recapture the easy, comfortable convictions he apparently held at this time.

However, the principal reason for the move to Oxford was the need for the sons to acquire a high-quality education. As recently as 1881 the Corporation had conceded that: 'It has long been felt a reproach to the City of Oxford, of one of

Opposite: The Oxford City High School for Boys, opened in 1881, with (highly characteristic of Oxford) a foreground litter of bicycles. The school having moved elsewhere in the city, the building now belongs to Oxford University.
Author photograph

the most ancient and famous of the Universities of Europe, that it has yet been absolutely without any recognized Grammar School for the sons of its citizens.' The timing could hardly have been more fortunate. In turn, and at relatively modest expense, the brothers acquired at the Oxford City High School For Boys the necessary skills and knowledge that would take them almost effortlessly to the university whose hallowed and ancient buildings were all around them. The school register which recorded the names of the young arrivals noted the name and profession of their father as 'Mr. T.R. Lawrence, gentleman of independent means', indicating that despite his severance from his original family he was still in receipt of sufficient funds to avoid having to turn to any paid occupation or trade. Indeed, he retained a substantial amount of capital as well as an annuity from the Chapman estates, thus allowing the family to pay not only for schooling, but also good clothes, family holidays, maids, even – by a nice irony – a governess.

As if to underline their confidence in their new situation, the parents did not overly try to merge their youngsters into the crowd but sent them to school in distinctive dark blue-and-white striped jerseys, probably Breton fishing jerseys, cheap, hard-wearing and with the advantage that they could be passed from brother to brother. These, according to one fellow-pupil, T.W. Chaundy, became 'almost a uniform, the softness of the wool matching a certain gentleness of speech and fairness of face'.

The inevitable question arises: did the alleged Mr and Mrs Lawrence convince their neighbours that they were a genuine married couple living a perfectly normal life?

One witness who believed they did not was the future Sir Basil Blackwell, from the family which founded Oxford's best known bookshop, a classmate of

Ned's at the City School. He would later talk of the Lawrences as being 'ostracized', as having 'something odd' about them, Oxford being 'very correct in those days', while acknowledging that even by Oxford standards 'they were so punctilious, churchgoing and water-drinking'. However, another schoolmate and neighbour, A.H.G. Kerry, speaking in the 1960s, had no such suspicions; indeed his memory of the Lawrences was largely a warm and engaging one: 'I remember father and mother and the five boys very well because we lived in the same road; I remember father generally dressed in a Norfolk jacket and breeches, and always waving cheerfully to us. He looked very like Bernard Shaw in fact, and he was a very courtly old gentleman. Mother I didn't see quite so much of, but I knew the four elder boys quite well.'

Asked 'What was the atmosphere like in the home?' Kerry answered: 'It was very like an ordinary suburban North Oxford home', while adding that the boys were 'very strictly brought up'. However, to the question, 'Did the family mix much socially?', he replied: 'I should have said not. No.'

How did T.E. Lawrence react to his situation? Indeed, what did he know, and when did he know? In a letter to Mrs George Bernard Shaw written from India in 1927, he would claim: 'I knew it before I was ten... and didn't care a straw', though he added that he did not learn the facts from his parents – 'they never told me' – rather, it appears, he worked things out for himself. He would also joke, in a letter of 1926 to his friend Lionel Curtis, that 'bars sinister [strictly 'bends sinister', the heraldic tokens of bastardy] are rather jolly ornaments; you feel so like a flea in the legitimate prince's bed'. But there is some evidence, as will be discussed at its proper place in the story, that the mark of illegitimacy went deeper than he outwardly acknowledged; that, indeed, he was left with a distinct if rarely articulated desire to reach back beyond the sad tale of outlaw

Not surprisingly, Lawrence was a man who unfolded himself slowly and carefully in the presence of strangers.

parents permanently wedded to deception, and to grasp the social respectability that he felt had been denied him – in effect to reclaim his lost birthright.

One other, perhaps widely underestimated, consequence of becoming aware of his own suspect origin was that he seems – consciously or unconsciously – to have adopted from quite early on what might be called techniques of cover-up, almost of evasion, which he could resort to as occasion required. Not surprisingly, Lawrence was a man who unfolded himself slowly and carefully in the presence of strangers. Thus E.H.R. Altounyan, surgeon and poet who met him in Syria and later became a fervent admirer, wrote of being repelled at first by what he called Lawrence's 'shut-up Oxford face, the downcast eyes, the soft reluctant speech', all of which he saw as suggesting 'a poseur'. Clearly he interpreted Lawrence's posing as a mixture of academic reserve and intellectual arrogance, when very possibly what had actually been disturbing him was the ingrained wariness of a man with something to hide.

Another hint that his background cut deep is, surely, to be found in two striking phrases that followed his 'didn't care a straw' disclaimer in the letter to Mrs Shaw quoted above. In an almost scathing comment on his parents he referred to 'the uprooting of their lives and principles' and then added, unequivocally: 'They should not have borne children'. This tallies remarkably with an old Greek epitaph he quoted in a letter written just weeks before his death: 'Here lie I of Tarsus, Never having married, and would that my father had not.'

As we know, *his* father had not married his mother, but the sentiment behind the quotation is quite clear. It is unusual, surely, for anyone granted so many natural gifts, with such outstanding ambition and so much to live for, to rue the fact that he had ever been born. Yet such a man was T.E. Lawrence.

2

His favoured sports were
unconventional, even at times
distinctly dangerous, such as
canoeing up the flooded River
Cherwell in winter – an escapade
in which he almost drowned.

Education of an adventurer

Despite the foregoing, it is evident that young Ned Lawrence had many more immediate things on his mind during his teenage years than contemplating his unusual personal background; indeed, it would be wrong to suggest other than that for most of the time he was a lively, fully focused youth pursuing a wide range of interests and enthusiasms.

He enjoyed a successful, though hardly meteoric, school career, did very respectably in examinations, but was not a 'blood', conventional sports having no appeal. Lawrence's only known contact with England's most celebrated if enigmatic team-game was a mocking article on playground cricket, contributed to the school magazine of July 1904 when he was fifteen. It included the following absurdities, hinting at something more like Eton's notorious no-holds-barred Wall Game than cricket's normally sedate rituals of white flannels and immaculate turf, with genteel applause as the red leather ball is stroked elegantly to the boundary:

Playground cricket has no handbook, so I think that some hints to youngsters who aspire to gain honours in this subject will be acceptable… A cap will not do for the ball. It can however be a stone, or a piece of wood: I have even seen a potato used with success. One man bats, another forty or so bowl… The forty boys scrimmage for the balls, and a game of Rugby football is played, till one gets hold of it and bowls at the stumps… The balls go, some into the side windows of the school, some through those of the factory, others again attach themselves to the windows opposite.

His favoured sports were unconventional, even at times distinctly dangerous, such as canoeing up the flooded River Cherwell in winter – an escapade in which he almost drowned – or making the dare-devil passage of Oxford's underground watercourse, the Trill Mill Stream. He also took up serious out-of-school hobbies, which, as it turned out, would stand him in good stead in his future career. One

notable enthusiasm, apparently acquired before he was ten, enjoyed a new phase of energetic creativity when he invited a schoolmate called C.F.C. ('Scroggs') Beeson, to accompany him on brass-rubbing expeditions to some of the churches in the surrounding countryside. Beeson, to whom Lawrence had previously seemed a rather quiet boy attracting little notice, happily responded and the two became for some years almost inseparable. There are hints that at times their searches took on a certain ruthlessness, with ancient pews or carpets being dragged aside to disclose brasses not easily accessible. Defending their actions Beeson noted: 'No damage was done so far as I know, although certain irate incumbents wrote to the newspapers and said vandals had appeared.' Meanwhile, high-quality brass-rubbings of medieval knights and other such worthies decorated the walls of Lawrence's bedroom at 2 Polstead Road.

A new passion soon seized them in Oxford itself, as they took advantage of the spate of building and rebuilding in the city at that time to assemble a collection of objects and artefacts garnered from the ground, of which a selection can still be seen in Oxford's internationally famous Ashmolean Museum. They became frequent visitors to the various diggings, offering threepence or sixpence to the workmen for any suitable specimens. They found appreciative recipients of their findings in two of the Ashmolean's Assistant Keepers, C.F. Bell, and, later, E.T. Leeds, their labours being handsomely acknowledged in the Museum's report for 1906: 'During the past year, considerable disturbance of the ground for the foundations of new buildings in the city... [has] produced many remains of pottery and glass of the sixteenth and seventeenth centuries. Owing to the generosity of Mr. E. Lawrence and Mr. C.F. Beeson who have by incessant watchfulness secured everything of antiquarian value which has been found, the most interesting finds have been added to the local antiquities in the Museum.'

A brass-rubbing made by Lawrence at Ewelme Parish Church, Oxfordshire, of Thomas Broke, Serjeant-at-Arms to King Henry VIII. All such brass-rubbings were followed by serious research in libraries into the history of the individual concerned.
Courtesy of Philip Kerrigan

Visits to London to explore its celebrated Norman Tower expanded their interest in related subjects such as armour and heraldry, while what would become for Lawrence a life-long fascination with fine printing began with a scheme devised together with Beeson to produce an edition of Froissart's *Chronicles* illustrated only by contemporary art. While enthusing over their crazes they could also mock them. Now it was Beeson's turn to play the humorist as he offered the school magazine an advertisement for a High School *Hysterical History of the World*, to appear in 170 elaborately bound volumes containing 'thousands of articles from the pens of competent historians both contemporaneous and cosmopolitan'. One proposed article which sounded almost serious was to be 'The development of pottery in Western Oxford'; its author, less seriously titled, was to be 'Prof. Lawrence'.

About this time Lawrence appears to have run away from home to serve as a boy-soldier in the Royal Garrison Artillery in Cornwall. The reason for this is unknown, but if it suggests a variant of the Dick Whittington theme of a young man adventurously seeking his fortune, it was not an escape with a happy outcome. Nothing had prepared him for the military low-life into which he found himself suddenly thrust. He later reported much 'ordeal of fists' and 'mass-bullying of anyone unlike the mass', adding: 'I cannot remember a parade… without a discoloured eye… The other fellows fought all Friday and Saturday nights and frightened me with their roughness'. It would seem that an appeal to his father resulted in his being hurriedly bought out.

The minute-book of the Oxford City High School helps to pin-point the likely date of this curious side-step by recording that on 30 April 1906 the Governing Body gave Thomas Edward Lawrence permission to stay on for another year, presumably because of the setback to his studies caused by his absence. Its cause is more difficult to define; references he made at least twice to 'trouble at home' are too vague to suggest anxiety about the family's status as a possible reason. Writing to his biographer Liddell Hart in the 1930s, he commented: 'This is hush-hush. I should not have told you… I'd rather keep this out of print, please: the whole episode.' His mother and elder brother later denied anything of the kind had taken place, but then they would not have wanted to give credence to an event which might cast doubts, however obliquely, on their message to the world that the home life of T.E. Lawrence had been notable throughout for its harmony and contentment.

Summer adventures provided the best antidote to any teenage traumas and there were plenty of them in the Lawrence family, all reported in breezy letters frequently laced with family jokes and badinage. In August 1905 a bicycle tour of East Anglia with his father produced a letter to his mother which included the injunction to 'kindly take heaps of love' for herself and divide the remainder among the 'worms' she had with her –. 'worms' being his standard term for his brothers, as well as a form of greeting, as in 'accept my best worms', while 'Worm' remained an affectionate name for the Benjamin of the family, Arnold, well into his teens. He also urged his mother to tell 'Beadle', his nickname for his brother Will, that the Norwich Museum contained the largest collection of birds of prey in existence, '409 out of 470 species'; then added, teasingly: 'I wonder if

'The Château Gaillard was so magnificent, and the postcards so abominable, that I stopped there an extra day, and did nothing but photograph, from 6 a.m. to 7 p.m... Its plan is marvellous, the execution wonderful, and the situation perfect.'

he'll shriek with horror when he hears that I did not look at them but went off and examined the Norman W.C.s.'

August 1906 found him in Brittany, travelling with his Polstead Road neighbours, the Kerrys, and 'Scroggs' Beeson. That year he bought postcards by which to remember the places he visited, but in 1907 – the year of his long-dreamed-of visit to Mont St Michel – he had his own camera, which was particularly valuable where postcards were unavailable or not up to scratch, as when he visited Richard the Lionheart's stunning castle at Les Andelys overlooking the River Seine:

The Château Gaillard was so magnificent, and the postcards so abominable, that I stopped there an extra day, and did nothing but photograph, from 6 a.m. to 7 p.m... Its plan is marvellous, the execution wonderful, and the situation perfect. The whole construction bears the unmistakable stamp of genius. Richard I must have been a far greater man than we usually consider him; he must have been a great strategist and a great engineer, as well as a great man-at-arms.

October 1907 marked a major step in Lawrence's education. He left the Oxford City High School for the University, becoming an undergraduate of Jesus College. Jesus was a foundation with Welsh connections and it was by virtue of his birth in Wales that he was able successfully to apply for a Meyricke Exhibition, with an annual value of £40. In the event he spent more time living at home than in college, though when he was in rooms there he rapidly acquired the reputation of an eccentric. Hence this comment by a veteran Honorary Fellow of the College, A.G. Prys-Jones, in the Jesus College Record of 1986. One year junior to Lawrence, he had met him in the rooms of a mutual friend and had invited him to pay a visit, which Lawrence shortly did:

*A minute or two after he had left, a very normal, intimate friend of mine dropped in.
He was a typical rowing and rugger man of the old school, a stalwart upholder of tradition
and correctness in all things, superlatively honest, dependable and loyal. In his blunt Anglo-
Saxon way he said 'I've just passed that lunatic Lawrence on the staircase. What's he been
doing on our territory?' 'Seeing me' I replied. 'My God, Prys, the man's barmy. Don't you
know that?' 'Well' I said 'either that or some kind of genius. I can't tell yet. Give me time,
old man: I've only just met him.'*

*'You Welshmen do seem to have the knack of picking the queerest fish. He doesn't
run with the boats, he doesn't play anything. He just messes about on that awful drop-
handled bicycle. And if he ever wore a bowler hat he'd wear it with brown boots.' 'Well, well,'
I said, 'that of course is perfectly dreadful. But he's got the most charming manners, probably
a first-class brain, and he's most refreshingly out of the ordinary...'*

*After that I got to know Lawrence pretty well, he would drop into my rooms casually
at any time. During the time of our friendship I never saw him eat a single solid meal.
The utmost he seemed capable of in the food line was to nibble at a few biscuits, a piece
of chocolate or a handful of raisins. I never understood how he retained his extraordinary
physical vitality on such meagre rations.*

Somewhat to the surprise of his fellow undergraduates Lawrence joined the
University Officers' Training Corps. However, as Prys-Jones recalls, he was not
its smartest member: 'He never seemed able to get his puttees wound correctly,
and the hang of his uniform showed considerable eccentricity.' It was a
characteristic that would irritate some of his superiors in the early stages of
the desert war. Despite his outwardly unsoldierly manner, he proved himself an
excellent marksman and scout, and showed no exhaustion after even the most
strenuous route-march.

When not in college he was based a five-minute bicycle ride away at Polstead Road, living not with the family but in his own special sanctum, a custom-built two-room bungalow erected in the garden, complete with water, electricity, fire-grate, even a telephone to the house. Perhaps it was his bid for independence by joining the Army that persuaded his parents to allow him a looser rein at home. He hung the walls with green cloth to emphasize the place's quiet serenity. Here, with a slowly dying fire, he could study far into the night, and then 'after wandering for hours in the forest with Percivale or Sagramors le desirious' he could 'open the door, and from over the Cherwell… look at the sun glowering through the valley mists'. The quotations are from a letter he wrote to his mother from France in 1910 about his passion for reading, especially alone, especially at night, when '… if you can get the right book at the right time you taste joys – not only bodily, physical, but spiritual also, which pass one out and beyond one's miserable self, as it were through a huge air, following the light of another man's thought. And you can never be quite the old self again.'

His chosen 'school' of study at Jesus College was history, in which he was to win the distinction of a brilliant first-class honours degree. He made this outcome virtually unassailable, by choosing as the theme of his dissertation a subject on which he became an unrivalled expert. Inevitably it was medieval and almost as inevitably it was about castles, but the idea of researching Crusader castles was a departure which took him, literally as well as in terms of scholarship, into new territory. The standard wisdom was that the castles of the Orient had been built largely after the styles then pertaining in Europe; he set out to prove the precise opposite. But he could only substantiate his argument by studying them in person. In the summer vacation of 1909 he applied to the illustrious

Lawrence's personal retreat in the garden of 2 Polstead Road, as seen from the house next door. Plans for the proposed building, described as 'Study and Bedroom for T. Lawrence Esq', were submitted to the Oxford City Council in October 1908.
Author collection

Lord Curzon, formerly Viceroy of India, then Chancellor of Oxford University, to use his good offices to acquire an *iradé* – an official authorisation from the Sultan – which would allow him to travel through Turkish territories. Equipped with this, a minimal backpack, and, vitally, a camera, he journeyed by train and sea to the Middle East, where he undertook an 1,100-mile walking tour through Syria and Palestine, in the course of which he worked at improving the Arabic he had begun learning at Oxford, almost lost his life to a gun-happy Arab and visited thirty-six out of fifty possible castles in the area of the Crusades. Delighting in a culture where English was not among the prevailing languages, he wrote to his mother from Latakia, on the Syrian coast, on 29 August:

I will have such difficulty in becoming English again, here I am Arab in habits and slip in talking from English to French and Arabic unnoticing: yesterday I was 3 hours with an Orleannais, talking French, and he thought at the end I was a 'compatriot'! How's that? Worms. Love

A further letter from Aleppo, announcing his immediate return for lack of money, contained a breezy reference to 'an absurd canard in the Aleppo paper of a week ago: my murder near Aintab (where I didn't go)... The hotel people received me like a ghost.'

He was late back for the university's Michaelmas Term. He asked his father to call at Jesus College to make his apologies, and he also wrote to the Principal, pleading 'four bouts of malaria when I had only reckoned on two'. A family friend described him on his return as 'thinned to the bone by privation'. Undeterred, on the contrary exalted by his experience and the quality of the evidence he had found, he worked hard at his thesis, entitled *The influence of the Crusades on European Military Architecture – to the end of the XIIth century*, which not only guaranteed his excellent degree but won him the academic advancement which would lead to the next major step in his career. D.G. Hogarth, the newly appointed Keeper of the Ashmolean Museum, procured for him a Senior Demyship (effectively a post-graduate scholarship carrying an emolument of £100 a year) at the college where he was a Fellow, Magdalen. This was not to enrol him as a member of the college's academic staff, but to

Crac des Chevaliers, one of the greatest
of Syria's Crusader Castles; Lawrence's
own adjective for it was 'tremendous'.
This is one of a number of striking
sketches he included in his university
thesis following his Middle Eastern
journey in 1909. From *Crusader Castles*,
by T.E. Lawrence.
The British Library, C98.i.14

finance his appointment to a major new archaeological dig being carried out
by the British Museum in Syria, at the ancient Hittite city of Carchemish on the
banks of the River Euphrates, with Hogarth as its leader. In a letter from Rouen
to E.T. Leeds, Lawrence announced his impending departure in characteristic
style: 'Mr Hogarth is going digging, and I am going out to Syria in a fortnight
to make plain the valleys and level the mountains for his feet: also to learn Arabic.
The two occupations fit into one another splendidly.'

It was November 1910. He would spend almost all of the next eight years
in the Orient.

3

'I walked through the door of the Parthenon... a heaviness in the air made my eyes swim, and wrapped up my senses: I only knew that I, a stranger, was walking on the floor of the place I had most desired to see...'

From Carchemish to Cairo

En route for Carchemish Lawrence spent more time than was originally envisaged on a steamship, the SS *Saghalien*, which suffered from faulty engines and kept on breaking down. Far from arousing his irritation this produced a series of remarkable bonuses, of which the first was a day in Naples – 'wonderfully beautiful' – while the second, even more gratifying, was an unscheduled visit to Athens. Two years earlier, after his memorable sighting of the Mediterranean, he had written that he would 'accept passage for Greece tomorrow'. Suddenly 'by extraordinary good fortune' he was there. As the ship limped into the harbour at Piraeus, the port for Athens, he was on deck and drinking it all in. In a letter home brimming with excitement, he wrote:

As we approached there gradually detached itself on the mainland from the mists a grey hill with black bars like cypresses upon the top. [Then] the sun rose, and like magic turned the black bars to gold, a wonderfully vivid gold of pillar and architrave and pediment, against the shadowed slopes of Hymettus. That was the Acropolis from a distance:- a mixture of all the reds and yellows you can think of with white for the highlights and brown-gold in the shadows.

In no time he was ashore and, having made his way through 'the intolerable cesspit' of Piraeus, found himself arriving at the Acropolis in an almost uncanny quiet: 'There were no porters, no guides, no visitors, and I walked through the door of the Parthenon, and on into the inner part of it, without really remembering where or who I was. A heaviness in the air made my eyes swim, and wrapped up my senses: I only knew that I, a stranger, was walking on the floor of the place I had most desired to see...'

As if this were not enough, the ship subsequently broke down for a whole week in Constantinople, affording another rich cultural experience – this time in

Previous page: Members of the
Carchemish work force; detail of a
photograph of 1913. In the front row,
left to right: Lawrence, facing camera;
Leonard Woolley, in charge of the
Carchemish dig from 1912; Fuad Bey,
site observer for the Imperial Ottoman
Museum; Sheikh Hamoudi, chief local
foreman, and Lawrence's close friend
and assistant, Dahoum.
British Museum

the principal city of his future enemies – so that he did not reach his first
intended destination until Christmas Eve 1909. This was the American Mission
school at Jebail, ancient Byblos, just north of Beirut in the Lebanon, where he
had stayed the previous year and where he was received almost as a returning son.
He remained there for two months, by the end of which he impressed his tutor,
Fareedeh el Akle, a Christian Syrian schoolmistress who would always number
him among her favourite pupils, by his ability to read, write and speak simple
Arabic. Yet, typically, his mind was not solely concentrated on his future task
as an archaeologist. A letter to his mother of 24 January 1911 discussed his long-
standing ambition, first developed with Beeson but now shared with a Jesus
College contemporary, Vyvyan Richards, to print fine books, while also
mentioning, almost casually, his plan to write two substantial books with links
to the Orient. One was what he described as 'my monumental work on the
Crusades'; the other would be a book about seven eastern cities. The plan for this
work was rudimentary, and it would never get beyond a draft which he burned
in 1914, but he had already selected its title. It would be called, after a text in the
Bible's Book of Proverbs, *The Seven Pillars of Wisdom*.

In late February 1911 Hogarth and his Cypriot foreman, Gregori, arrived
in Beirut to accompany Lawrence to Carchemish. A winter storm that produced
the worst snows for forty years closed the mountain road to Damascus, so
they were forced to take a circuitous route via northern Palestine. They visited
Mount Carmel, and, if from a distance, saw Nazareth, which Lawrence thought
considerably less enchanting than Naples. If viewed from a certain hilltop,
however, 'it is then no uglier than Basingstoke, or very little, and the view from it,
southwards over the plain, is beautiful.' Travelling eastwards via the Yarmuk Valley
they joined the recently built Hejaz Railway, devised to carry pilgrims to and

The cultural omens were promising. Summing up their joint literary library, he told his mother: 'Thompson has a complete Shakespeare, Mr. Hogarth a Dante and some French novels, and I a complete Spenser'.

from the Islamic holy city of Mecca, which was to become the prime target of Lawrence's wartime raids. The journey included a lunch for three in the station buffet at Deraa, a town that would also have a memorable role in his wartime experiences. By 1 March he was writing from Aleppo: 'We reached here last night, over a snow-covered line from Damascus: nothing of note'; Damascus too would have considerably greater resonance for him in later years.

Another archaeologist, R. Campbell Thompson, was waiting at Aleppo to join the team. The cultural omens were promising. Summing up their joint literary library, he told his mother: 'Thompson has a complete Shakespeare, Mr. Hogarth a Dante and some French novels, and I a complete Spenser'. They took rooms for nine days in Aleppo's Baron's Hotel, collecting food and equipment for the expedition.

While at Aleppo they were regularly entertained by the British Consul, R.A. Fontana and his wife Winifred. She was to become one of Lawrence's warmest admirers, but only after piercing an initial barrier that she found quite disturbing. Essentially her experience was not dissimilar to that noted by E.H.R. Altounyan, though she put it in stronger language: 'Something uncouth in Lawrence's manner contrasting with a donnish manner of speech, chilled me.' She shrewdly discerned, however, that one cause at least of his behaviour was the instinctive awkwardness of someone unfamiliar with accepted social codes. When he refused an invitation to dine because he had no dress-clothes to wear, she overcame his reluctance and persuaded him to attend. She would later write: 'This was possibly the first brick in the foundations of our subsequent friendly relation.'

On 11 March the party, by this time a rather larger one than the four individuals who had assembled at Aleppo, arrived at its destination. Lawrence immediately wrote home: 'We have got here, and this is a hurried note to go off

Opposite: An article in the *Illustrated London News* on the excavations at Carchemish, published in January 1914; text by D.G. Hogarth, photographs by T.E. Lawrence. The dig would be halted later that year following the outbreak of war.
BL Newspaper Library, Colindale

by the returning camel men... Not much yet of course to say about this place. The mounds are enormous: but I'll send you a photo, or drawing later. We only got in about 4 o'clock: and have been unpacking since: eleven baggage horses, ten camels...'

His years at Carchemish were to affect his life and career in numerous ways. His responsibilities for organising the locally recruited labour force helped promote in him an understanding of the 'rank and file': life's canon fodder whether in peace or war – an insight which would later make it possible, almost though never entirely, to become one of them himself. He would also acquire an acute insight into the Oriental mind and an awareness of what he perceived as a genuine if half-formed desire on the part of the native peoples to win freedom from Turkish rule, this being part of the territory of the Ottoman Empire, whose alliance with Germany in the coming war would create the circumstances that would offer him his great opportunity. Thus he gained a 'cause' which would sustain him, though also torment him, for much of the rest of his life.

He would always look back with great affection on his time here. Altounyan, whom he met at the site in 1911, recorded him as saying a decade or so later: 'I haven't had much kick out of life; those days in Carchemish were the best'. That he thought so then is clear from a letter he wrote to his 'small brother' Arnold, whom he addressed not as 'Worm' but as 'Ancient Beast': 'It is about a year since we wrote letters to one another: suppose we do it again? It doesn't cost anything but time, and of time do you know, I have mints just now. This is the first time for years and years that I have been able to sit down and think, and it is so precious a discovery: and one that so many people want to take from you.'

There have been theories to the effect that Lawrence mixed espionage with archaeology at this period, the assumption being that he spent at least some of his

REVEALING THE CIVILISATION OF THE HITTITES OF SYRIA: EXCAVATIONS AT CARCHEMISH.

OF THE LATER PERIOD (EIGHTH-SEVENTH CENTURY): A BACK VIEW OF A HEAD WEARING A TURBAN, FOUND AT THE SOUTH-WEST GATE.

CARCHEMISH.

THE FINEST HITTITE WORK YET DISCOVERED AT JERABLUS, WHERE ONCE STOOD CARCHEMISH: THREE MALE HEADS FROM A BROKEN DOLERITE RELIEF.

A FRAGMENT OF A STATUE IN DOLERITE: A HITTITE OF THE PEOPLES WHOSE HISTORY IS BEING OPENED UP FOR US.

THREE years ago the Trustees of the British Museum undertook what has proved the largest, and in many respects the most important and fruitful, excavation which they have ever promoted. When the enterprise was in the initial stage, in which I myself and Mr. Campbell Thompson conducted it, I wrote in these columns a preliminary notice, giving the history and a description of the site at Jerablus, where the work had been begun, and indulging in a little prophecy of our hopes. Now three years have seen six campaigns in the soil on which there is no reasonable doubt once stood Carchemish, the leading city among the Hittite peoples of Syria. Mr. C. L. Woolley, well known for his Nubian researches, and Mr. T. E. Lawrence, who worked under Mr. Thompson and myself, have been in charge for the most part of this time, carrying on the excavation for a spring season and an autumn season in each year with between two and three hundred men. They have had their difficulties, and even their dangers, for Jerablus lies in a lawless region, among Kurdish tribes excited by recent events in Turkey; but they have faced and surmounted them with courage, persistence, and signal use of the faculty which so many Britons possess for gaining the confidence of wild fighting folk. By the end of next spring season the Trustees, who have been splendidly supported by private munificence, will have expended some £10,000 on the site; but the work, which is opening up Hittite history for us, and the nature of the civilisation occupying the geographical space between the Semites and the Hellenes, will not be much more than half done. In the hope that the completion of this British enterprise will not have to be resigned to alien hands (if we do not finish it, the German scholars who follow up the Baghdad Railway, now running to Jerablus, will surely do so ; and, failing us, more power to

staff, and a baby in the arms of a woman, who leads a pet animal. She should be the Queen, who appears nowhere else in the group. The children throw knuckle-bones or carry whipping-tops according to sex and age. In front of the whole group is a hieroglyphic inscription, the longest known, which, with the legends graven near the head of each member of the group, would tell us who they all were, could we read the script. We can, however, guess safely that it is a royal group of about the ninth century B.C.

The style and execution of these reliefs upset all our previous ideas about the quality of Hittite art; as do also the sculptures which line the opposite side of the portal—royal ministers and servants in whose delineation has been used a grace which is almost Greek. Of the soldiers who follow them—note their "Carian" helmets, as the Greeks would have thought—of the long file of priestesses and acolytes bearing animals for sacrifice, of the slabs of mythologic scenes beyond the soldiers, and of the other inscribed inner doorways, we can give only two or three specimen views. As excavation proceeds, this great series of sculptures will no doubt be found to be prolonged at either end.

From this building a wall, also bearing reliefs along all its length, runs up to a great staircase, which climbs up the face of the Acropolis, and is (or was) lined with sculptures of which some are still in position. To the left is another building of the palatial complex built on the terraced slope. Here was found a small, shrine-like chamber with elaborately inscribed portal, before which stood a great laver, supported, like Solomon's, by two bulls, which are shown in one of our views.

On the Acropolis the remains are less well-preserved because in Roman days a great temple was built there,

FROM THE DADO OF MYTHOLOGIC SLABS: A HUMAN AND LION-HEADED SPHINX WITH TAIL ENDING IN A BIRD'S HEAD.

B.C., perhaps, the lords of Carchemish were Aramaean Semites. Our view gives the back of the head to show the turban-like dress worn by the figure. The North Gate, of still more elaborate construction and plan, is still under excavation.

Within the walls a large complex of Hittite palatial buildings has been partially cleared, together with a water-gate on the river bank which was flanked by great lions in dolerite, inscribed with Hittite hieroglyphic texts. The westernmost member of this complex is a large building entered by a portal from both jambs of which run, as far as the clearance has yet been made, dadoes of sculptured slabs, alternately of black dolerite and white limestone. The finest reliefs, those of the façade of the portal itself, show two men, probably two Kings, one being really, followed by eight children, of whom the last still totters, holding to

PROBABLY OF BETWEEN 2000 AND 1500 B.C.: VASES OF THE PECULIAR FORM CHARACTERISTIC OF THE EARLY CIST GRAVES.

their elbow!) the Trustees permit me to put before your readers.

The site consists of what is called a "royal city"; that is, a strongly fortified enclosure containing palaces and their appurtenances, with a citadel, and an unfortified area inhabited by the commons. It is the first which is being explored. Its ring-wall, which enclosed about half a square mile on the bank of the Euphrates, has been stripped away to build a later town; but the huge mound on which the wall stood still remains, rising from the moat to a height, in places, of nearly fifty feet. Also three gates remain, of which two have been explored. Here, under Hellenistic and Roman structures, the explorers have laid bare remains of Hittite buildings, consisting of flanking towers and successive lion-guarded portals, one within another, divided by open courts, in each of which an enemy, breaking in, would have had to encounter flanking fire. The fine masonry of the south-west gate is well shown in one of our views, in which the spectator looks outwards over the plain on which Nebuchadnezzar settled accounts with Pharaoh Necho in 605 B.C. Now it is diversified by the line, sheds, and other constructions of the Baghdad Railway. In excavating this gate, the explorers found a fine head of a god or king of the latest Hittite Age, when, in the seventh century

FOUND ON THE CITADEL OF THE STRONGLY FORTIFIED "ROYAL CITY": A COLUMN BASE SUPPORTED BY TWO LIONS.

whose foundations almost destroyed the large brick buildings of the Hittites. At the north end, too, Sargon the Assyrian, who captured Carchemish in 717 B.C., built a residence for his officer. This has been cleared and its remains appear in one of our photographs, which looks northwards up the Euphrates. But the Acropolis has yielded a most important set of early tombs, with which we can now compare the contents of another cemetery outside the walls.

From Jerablus and its neighbourhood we have a long series of graves which show us the pottery and implements and seals of the Syrian Hittites from about 2000 to about 1500 B.C.; and when it is said, in conclusion, that the stratification of the city site gives us orderly evidence from the Neolithic Age to the close of the Bronze Age; that the development of Hittite plastic art can now be studied from its cradle to its grave; that the same is true of the hieroglyphic script, of which over a hundred new texts have come to light; that we have cuneiform inscriptions already, and may at any moment get a bilingual key to the hieroglyphic puzzles—when so much can be said for three years' work on a part only of this great site, it will be agreed that it is well worth digging completely. D. G. HOGARTH.

LEADING UP TO THE CITADEL: THE LOWER PART OF THE GREAT STAIRWAY.
Some of the bordering sculptures of this were found in 1879 and sent to the British Museum.

Opposite: The living room of the
archaeologists' house at Carchemish,
richly furnished with carpets and other
objects acquired from dealers in Aleppo
and elsewhere and suggesting a habitat
distinctly less than Spartan.
Photograph by Lawrence, 1913.
British Museum

'mints' of time scrutinising the Berlin–Baghdad Railway currently being built
by German engineers in the vicinity of Carchemish. A. W. Lawrence, his youngest
brother and after T.E.'s death the custodian of his reputation, always strongly
denied that he was an actual spy while admitting that archaeologists and similar
field workers, indeed, any serious British traveller in distant parts, might be
expected to keep their eyes open and could be asked about their findings.
His summing up of the Carchemish years was brief and pithy: 'I think T.E.
was mainly enjoying himself.'

The work itself was exhilarating; it was what he had dreamed of and there
were no examinations at the end of the season. He applied himself diligently if
with a certain wayward exuberance, for he was not always the most systematic of
archaeologists and could easily irritate his more academically minded colleagues.
There was also the prospect, as opportunity offered, of adventure. In the summer
of 1911 he set off on a typically Lawrencian journey, one aim of which was to
continue his study of Crusader castles, recording his experiences in an often
eloquent diary and through a clutch of remarkable photographs. During the
walk he suffered agonies from toothache and came back from it weakened by
dysentery, an attack serious enough to require some months of convalescence
in England. Soon after returning to Carchemish in December, at Hogarth's
suggestion, he left for Egypt to gain further experience under the celebrated
Egyptologist, Flinders Petrie. He was impressed by his new chief but soon found
that disinterring mummified bodies – 'dark brown, fibrous, visibly rotting' – was
not to his liking, nor did he enjoy the tensions and rivalries among Petrie's camp-
followers. He was much relieved to be back in Carchemish for the start of a new
digging season in March 1912.

Hogarth, whose duties at the Ashmolean did not sort easily with fieldwork,

was no longer in charge, while Thompson had returned home to marry and Lawrence now found himself number two to Leonard Woolley, eight years his senior, who by his later discovery of the royal tombs of Ur was to become one of the world's most renowned archaeologists. Woolley had himself been briefly at the Ashmolean and remembered Lawrence as the eager schoolboy bearing gifts, and was therefore happy to retain his services when Hogarth departed. We owe to him a fascinating, if mixed, portrait of Lawrence at this time:

From the outset he was excellent with the Arab workmen. In a way he was rather like them, for the fun of the thing appealed to him as much as did its scientific interest. It was he who invented the system whereby a discovery was saluted by revolver-shots carefully proportioned to its importance; the men competed together as to who should have the greatest number of shots to his credit in the course of a season, and the hope of a few more cartridges was the chief incitement to hard work.

Lawrence had a close ally in managing the workforce in the person of Sheikh Hamoudi, born at Carchemish and chief local foreman on the dig. Together, as Woolley put it, the Syrian and the Englishman '… would suddenly turn the whole work into a game, the pick-men pitted against the basket-men or the entire gang against the wagon-boys, until with two hundred men running and yelling half a day's output would be accomplished in an hour; and Lawrence would lead the yells.'

Lawrence acquired another, much younger Arab friend at this time: Dahoum – not an actual name but a nickname, meaning 'the Dark One', a reference to his unusually dusky complexion. Woolley wrote of him:

He was then a boy of about fifteen, not particularly intelligent (though Lawrence taught him to take photographs quite well) but beautifully built and remarkably handsome. Lawrence was devoted to him. The Arabs were tolerantly scandalized by the friendship, especially when in 1913 Lawrence, stopping in the house after the dig was over, had Dahoum to live with him and got him to pose as model for a queer crouching figure which he carved in the soft local limestone and set up on the edge of the house roof; to make an image was bad enough in its way, but to portray a naked figure was proof to them of evil of another sort. The scandal about Lawrence was widely spread and firmly believed.

The charge was quite unfounded. Lawrence had in his make-up a very strong vein of sentiment, but he was in no sense a pervert; in fact, he had a remarkably clean mind. He was tolerant, thanks to his classical reading, and Greek homosexuality interested him, but in a detached way, and the interest was not morbid but perfectly serious...

He knew quite well what the Arabs said about himself and Dahoum and so far from resenting it was amused, and I think that he courted misunderstanding rather than tried to avoid it; it appealed to his sense of humour, which was broad and schoolboyish. He liked to shock.

It is also important to add that when, years later, Lawrence dedicated *Seven Pillars of Wisdom* to 'S.A', in a remarkable poem beginning with the lines: 'I loved you, so I drew these tides of men into my hands/and wrote my will across the sky in

A light-hearted experiment in wearing
Arab clothes; Lawrence, left, in
headdress and outer garments
borrowed from Dahoum, right.
Photographed by the two sitters,
c. 1912.
*The British Library, Add. MS 50584
ff.116, 115*

stars/To earn you Freedom, the seven pillared worthy house…' – the general
assumption has increasingly identified 'S.A.' as 'Sheikh Ahmed', the alleged actual
name of Dahoum. Boy friend? Good companion and personal symbol of an
emergent nation? Bearing in mind Lawrence's extreme fastidiousness and
Woolley's powerful disclaimer, the balance is far more in favour of the second
interpretation than the first.

Realising from his unhappy experience in 1911 that it was not always
sensible to travel alone, he took Dahoum with him on a number of journeys, at
times even resorting to wearing Arab clothes, which attracted less attention and,
as he would later claim, were 'cleaner and more decent in the desert'. Even more

Opposite: A photograph taken by
Lawrence, during the Sinai expedition
of early 1914, of a Byzantine cistern at
Biz Berein, with Dahoum on its far side
to provide a sense of scale. One place of
considerable future interest he visited
at this time was the port of Akaba, at
the northern end of the Red Sea.
*Courtesy Palestine Exploration Fund,
London*

daringly, in 1913, he decided to offer Hamoudi and Dahoum a brief holiday
in Oxford, the trio living together in Lawrence's bungalow in the garden at
2 Polstead Road. Equipped, for practical reasons, with ladies' bicycles, they created
a modest sensation as they cycled in their flowing robes through the Oxford
streets, while, for their part, they were duly amazed during a visit to the capital
to encounter the sights and sounds of the London Underground.

Life at Carchemish was soon to be interrupted by a mission which had
a profound effect on Lawrence's career. In January 1914 he and Woolley were
invited to join a survey along the Egyptian border between the Mediterranean
and the Red Sea in Turkish-held territory which had been called for by the
Director of Military Operations in London, against the possibility – in the event
of war – of a Turkish offensive in the direction of Britain's great imperial lifeline,
the Suez Canal. The survey was to be led by Captain Stewart Newcombe of the
Royal Engineers, but was to be conducted under the highly respectable auspices
of the Palestine Exploration Fund. This civilian cover was clearly essential;
without it, the Turkish authorities were hardly likely to sanction what was in
essence an exercise in military espionage. With Dahoum as aide and servant,
Woolley and Lawrence embarked on six weeks of strenuous travel, during which
Newcombe did his work and they did theirs. 'We are obviously only meant
as red herrings', Lawrence told his mother, 'to give an archaeological colour
to a political job.'

One special bonus for him was a visit to Petra, which inspired a spirited
account in a letter to his Oxford colleague E.T. Leeds, in which he described that
ancient city of the Nabateans as 'the most wonderful place in the world, not for
the sake of its ruins, which are quite a secondary affair, but for the colour of its
rocks... and the shape of its cliffs and crags and pinnacles, and for the wonderful

gorge it has, always running deep in spring-water, full of oleanders, and ivy and ferns, and only just wide enough for a camel at a time.' Familiarity with the East had not dulled his joy at its splendours.

He learned much from this episode. It was his first experience of collaborating with a professional soldier engaged in a military mission, and, moreover, one conducted inside enemy lines. By observing Newcombe at work, planning itineraries, interpreting maps, assessing terrain, as he, Lawrence, would do in the future, he was effectively undergoing a personal training course. There was a more immediate product, however, a report on his and Woolley's findings which duly appeared later that year under the title of *The Wilderness of Zin*. 'The filthiest manuscript made' was his verdict on it to Hogarth. 'Parts of the book are frivolous', he told Dr Cowley of the Bodleian Library, Oxford, 'so don't call it a

Previous pages: Petra, celebrated in a
famous description by the nineteenth-
century Victorian divine Dean Burgon,
as 'a rose red city, half as old as time'.
The opportunity to visit this ancient
capital of the Nabatean civilization was
for Lawrence a gratifying bonus of the
Sinai expedition.
Author photograph

"serious contribution".' But Lawrence was ever a fierce denigrator of his own
efforts and the report was widely acknowledged as a work of value and quality,
and all the more remarkable for being written, necessarily, at some speed. For by
the time it was concluded the world was at war, Lawrence after the briefest of
seasons had left Carchemish for good, Dahoum had faded from his life except
as a treasured memory – he would die, obscurely, of typhus before the war was
over – and Lawrence and Woolley were in military uniform. The latter 'wangled'
(Lawrence's term) a commission in the Royal Artillery, while he himself was
drawn into the Geographical Section of the General Staff (Intelligence) based in
the War Office in London. He arrived first as a civilian – hatless, in grey flannels,
and looking about eighteen, according to the Colonel who recruited him – but
by 26 October he was gazetted as a second lieutenant on the 'Special List', the
standard category for officers assigned to general duties and with no regimental
attachment.

By coincidence, Turkey entered the war as an ally of Germany and
Austria–Hungary just three days later. Before the year was out Lawrence was
on his way back to the east to join a newly formed Intelligence Department in
Cairo. Newcombe and, briefly, Woolley were members of it, as were *The Times*
correspondent Philip Graves, Père Jaussen, a French Dominican monk fluent
in Arabic, and two Members of Parliament with experience as attachés to
the British Embassy in Constantinople, George (later Lord) Lloyd and the
Honourable Aubrey Herbert. Perhaps the most eccentric among this small galaxy
were Herbert and Lawrence; Herbert, pre-war traveller and adventurer who
would become the first model for John Buchan's brilliant hero Sandy Arbuthnot
in *Greenmantle*, and Lawrence, who, in Buchan's later novel, *The Courts of the
Morning*, would become the second. The two surveyed each other curiously.

To Lawrence, Herbert was 'a joke, but a very nice one'. More trenchantly, when Herbert, describing in his diary the new gathering of talents, reached the short animated import from Oxford and Carchemish, he noted: 'And then there's Lawrence, an odd gnome, half cad – with a touch of genius'.

For a man who would become a war-hero, it can seem curious that he spent his first two years in uniform either in a map-room or behind a desk. 'We have no adventures, except with the pen,' he wrote to C.F. Bell of the Ashmolean in April 1915. 'I am going to be in Cairo till I die,' he informed a lady correspondent in February 1916: 'Yesterday I was looking over samples of pyramids at an undertaker's with a view to choosing my style. I like the stepped ones best.'

Pleasantries apart, there was a sharp edge to his frustration because 1915 had seen the death in action of two of his brothers. Frank had died first, in May, as a Second Lieutenant in the 1st Gloucesters, killed by shell fire when leading his men up to the line before an attack. Will died in October, shot down as an observer of the Royal Flying Corps having been in France for just one week. Writing to E.T. Leeds in November, Lawrence had admitted: 'I'm rather low because first one and now another of my brothers has been killed... They were both younger than I am, and it doesn't seem right, somehow, that I should go on living peacefully in Cairo.'

He was briefly in a war zone in March 1916 when he was sent with Aubrey Herbert to Mesopotamia to attempt to negotiate a satisfactory outcome to the siege of Kut-al-Amara on the River Tigris, where the 6th Division of the Indian Expeditionary Force, under Major-General Sir Charles Townshend, had been bottled up by a much larger Turkish force since the previous December. Blind-folded, the two men were taken through enemy lines, their hope being to achieve

their goal by offering an acceptable ransom, their only practical success being the
release of a handful of sick and wounded. Forced to surrender, Townshend was
consigned to a comparatively comfortable captivity in Constantinople, while
the bulk of his Command embarked on a horrific forced march to Turkey which
relatively few survived. On the way back to Cairo Lawrence wrote a report
condemning the deficiencies in the Indian Army's organisation and generalship
in Mesopotamia, which was substantially borne out by the inquiry which
Herbert won later that year from Parliament. The report was so forthright
that it was thought advisable to have it doctored before it was shown to the
Commander-in-Chief in Egypt, General Sir Archibald Murray.

As this minor chapter closed, a far greater one was about to open, one in
which, contrary to received assumptions, Lawrence had been deeply involved for
many months. His world-weary comments on the dullness of life in Cairo were
in fact a screen to cover much hard effort from the spring of 1915 onwards, the
purpose of which was to spread the virus of insurrection against Turkish rule.
For while the main struggle between the Allies and the Turks in the Middle East
would inevitably be between conventional armies fighting conventional battles,
there could be much advantage in promoting other smaller-scale initiatives to
discomfort and destabilise the enemy from inside his own territory. Responding
to the interest emanating from Cairo and bolstered by assurances of Allied
support, in June 1916 one of the great figures of the region, Grand Sherif Hussein
of Mecca, who enjoyed the huge prestige of being the guardian of Islam's most
sacred site, launched the Arab Revolt, thus opening a significant new phase in the
Middle Eastern war, and providing a certain young intelligence officer of high
ambition with the opportunity to exchange his desk in Egypt for what would
become a glittering if controversial career in the Arabian desert.

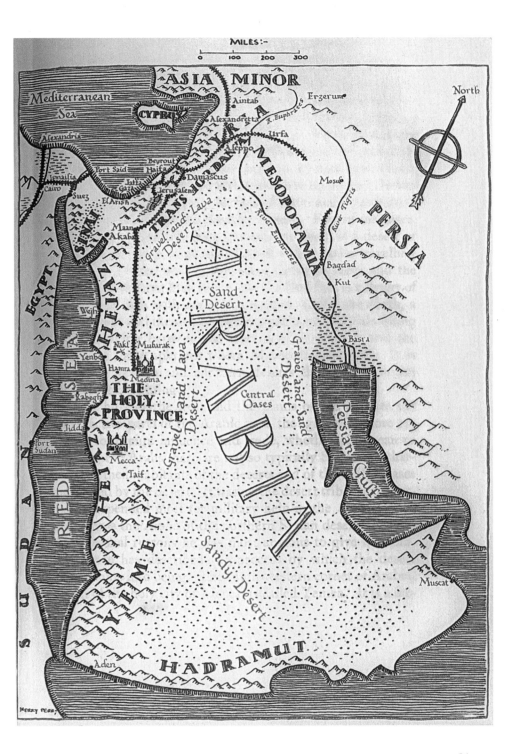

MILES :-

0   100   200   300

Mediterranean
Sea

ASIA MINOR

CYPRUS

Aintab

Alexandretta

Erzerum

North

Alexandria

Port Said
Ismailia
Cairo
Suez

Beyrout
Jaffa
Gaza
El Arish

Haifa

Damascus

Jerusalem

EGYPT

SINAI

Maan
Akaba

SYRIA

TRANS JORDANIA

R. Euphrates

Urfa

Aleppo

Mosul

MESOPOTAMIA

River Euphrates

River Tigris

PERSIA

Bagdad
Kut

Basra

Gravel and Lava Desert

ARABIA

Sand
Desert

Gravel and Sand Desert

Wejh

HEJAZ

Nakl
Hamra
Medina

THE
HOLY
PROVINCE

Mubarak

Yenbo

Rabegh

Jidda

Port
Sudan

Mecca

Taif

Gravel and Lava Desert

Central
Oases

Persian Gulf

SUDAN

RED SEA

HEJAZ

YEMEN

Sandy Desert

Muscat

Aden

HADRAMUT

MERRY PRESS

51

4

The desert war: the basis and the beginning

When Lawrence set out for Arabia in October 1916 he was an unknown of twenty-eight. What he achieved and experienced in the two years that followed would give him fame. It would also provide him with the 'plot' for the masterwork he had long dreamed of writing: 'I had had one craving all my life – for the power of self-expression in some imaginative form – but had been too diffuse ever to acquire a technique. At last accident, with perverted humour, in casting me as a man of action had given me place in the Arab Revolt, a theme ready and epic to a direct eye and hand, thus offering me an outlet in literature…'

This statement explains at a stroke why he would not be content to write an unassuming memoir of a kind that poured in thousands from the presses in the years following the First World War. Nothing would have been easier than to throw off a jaunty adventure yarn under such a title as – say – *By Camel and Armoured Car to Damascus*, or *Daring Days in the Desert*. Had he done so, his effort would have joined the long backlist of dusty volumes from that era that have been almost entirely forgotten, or nudge their way as old curiosities into the catalogues of the military booksellers.

By contrast, Lawrence wrote his account at prodigious length and gave it the high-sounding title of the book he had conceived but never written on eastern cities. In a Preface to the book, his brother, A.W. Lawrence, explained: 'The seven pillars of wisdom are first mentioned in the Bible, in the Book of Proverbs (ix.1). "Wisdom hath builded a house: she hath hewn out her seven pillars".'

Referring to his brother's earlier discarded work, he stated that 'he transferred the title as a memento'. Hence *Seven Pillars of Wisdom*.

Yet the title is no arbitrary one; it has its justification. The work consists of an Introduction and ten so-called 'Books' (originally the intended figure had been seven – seven pillars, seven parts – but that symmetry did not survive). The

Previous page: His Highness Hussein,
Emir and Sherif of Mecca. Frequently
referred to more simply as 'Grand Sherif
Hussein of Mecca', it was his
declaration of independence from the
Ottoman Empire in June 1916 that
started the Arab Revolt.
Imperial War Museum, Q 59888

Introduction is entitled 'Foundations of
Revolt'; the final book is headed 'The
House is Perfected'. Essentially, however,
the title is a kind of metaphor, a claim that
the story it would unfold was one of
consequence. If nothing else, it says, do not
ignore this work, it is worth your notice and
might well be worth your memory. As if to
raise its profile still further he gave it the
provocative subtitle *A Triumph*. In these
ways Lawrence was able to fix in the general
mind the cause for which he had fought
and make it unforgettable. Unlike the
majority of the memoirs earlier referred
to, it has never been out of print.

Yet the tale had to be lived before it
could be told. As in all the best stories, his
begins with a journey. Once again, this is
the young adventurer heading 'farther out' –
or rather in this case farther south, first from
Cairo to Suez by train, then on by ship in the S.S. *Lama*, his destination the Red
Sea port of Jidda on the Hejaz Peninsula. He would describe his arrival in Arabia
in a deliberately virtuoso piece of writing:

We had the accustomed calm run to Jidda, in the delightful Red Sea climate, never too hot
while the ship was moving. By day we lay in shadow; and for great part of the glorious

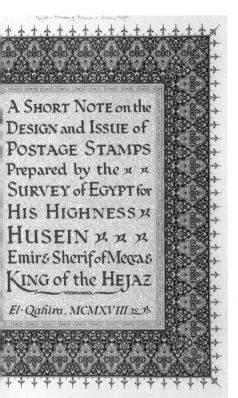

A SHORT NOTE on the DESIGN and ISSUE of POSTAGE STAMPS Prepared by the ⅀ ⅀ SURVEY of EGYPT for HIS HIGHNESS ⅀ HUSEIN ⅀ ⅀ ⅀ Emir & Sherif of Mecca & KING of the HEJAZ

El-Qahira, MCMXVIII

nights we would tramp up and down the wet decks under the stars in the steaming breath of the southern wind. But when at last we anchored in the outer harbour, off the white town hung between the blazing sky and its reflection in the mirage which swept and rolled over the wide lagoon, then the heat of Arabia came out like a drawn sword and struck us speechless. It was mid-day; and the noon sun in the East, like moonlight, put to sleep the colours. There were only lights and shadows, the white houses and black gaps of streets: in front, the pallid lustre of the haze shimmering upon the inner harbour: behind, the dazzle of league after league of featureless sand, running up to an edge of low hills, faintly suggested in the far away mist of heat.

This is, intentionally, a dramatic curtain-raiser, a striking scene-set: the heat-baked town in the foreground, the desert, where the action to come will be played, looming beyond. Yet the mission which took Lawrence for the first time to Arabia, was basically a routine intelligence task with few hints of heroics to come. The British in Cairo needed a first-hand appreciation of the progress of the Revolt, which appeared to have stalled. The Grand Sherif Hussein of Mecca had launched his campaign but had left it to his three elder sons, the Emirs Ali, Abdullah and Feisal, to get on with it.

Each had his own force, but each was operating independently with little cohesion. The British representative in Jidda, Colonel C.E. Wilson, had reported his unease to Cairo, and Lawrence's superior at Headquarters, Brigadier-General Clayton, had decided to send his young if somewhat unconventional captain, by this time an expert on Turkish forces and the geography of the region as well as an enthusiast for the Arab cause and a passable speaker of Arabic, to assess the situation at first hand.

He travelled in company with Ronald Storrs, Oriental Secretary at the British Agency in Egypt since 1909, who had acted as intermediary with the Grand Sherif in negotiations preceding the Revolt, and with whom Lawrence had recently collaborated in the designing and production of postage stamps to support the Arabs' claim for independence – a ruse made necessary by the Sherif's repudiation of his Turkish masters, but also a brilliant and, literally, a colourful propaganda coup. Storrs and Lawrence had scoured the Museums of Cairo to find appropriate designs, which they proposed should be conspicuously non-Ottoman in style by being based on 'beautiful existing specimens of Arabesque ornament'. Produced under Lawrence's close supervision in September, they appeared in October; it is characteristic of the commitment and enthusiasm of both men that they celebrated their arrival in the Hejaz by sending postcards to Cairo bearing the new stamps.

Hussein was not in Jidda to meet the new arrivals. He was unreachable in Mecca except, with difficulty, by telephone – his number being, as Lawrence indicated in an amused aside for his brother 'Arnie' in a home letter, 'No 1 Mecca'. However, the Sherif's second son Emir Abdullah was present in the town, and so he was the first of the leaders of the Revolt whom Lawrence encountered. Wilson and Storrs were the key negotiators, Lawrence mainly being an observer, but as an intelligence officer he was soon busy, writing 'personal notes' about their host, from which a vivid picture emerges of this notable

Whether Abdullah realised it or not, the small, intense third man of the British party was effectively putting him through a kind of examination...

Middle Eastern figure (later to become first ruler of the Hashemite Kingdom of Jordan) as he was in young middle-age:

In manner affectedly open and very charming, not standing at all on ceremony, but jesting with the tribesmen like one of their own sheikhs. On serious occasions he judges his words carefully, and shows himself a keen dialectician. Is probably not so much the brain as the spur of his father. He is obviously working to establish the greatness of the family, and has large ideas, which no doubt include his own particular advancement. The clash between him and Feisal will be interesting.

Whether Abdullah realised it or not, the small, intense third man of the British party was effectively putting him through a kind of examination, pursuing the goal, as much for his own purposes as for those of his Cairo mentors, of searching out the Arab leader best qualified to head the campaign against the Turks. It is clear that Lawrence had caveats about Abdullah, detecting a hint of vain-glory in him, a concern for himself as much as for the cause, while the reference to the 'clash' between him and his brother Feisal suggests that for the time being he was putting him on hold.

There was another important meeting in Jidda, when the British officers dined with Colonel Edouard Brémond, head of a French military mission which had been in the Hejaz since late September. Far from this being a pleasant social encounter, the occasion only served to underline what Lawrence had already acquired in Cairo – a deep distrust of French plans and motives, sensing that Britain's principal ally in Europe was likely to prove more of a rival in the Middle East, with views on the future of the region totally opposed to his own. As he saw it, France wanted for herself what Lawrence was now ever more firmly wanting for the Arabs. This merely steeled his resolve.

Opposite: Emir Feisal was the third of the four sons of the Grand Sherif, but was seen by Lawrence as the most capable and inspirational leader to emerge out of the Arab Revolt. This portrait, painted by Augustus John in 1919, became the frontispiece to the 1926 'subscribers' edition' of Lawrence's *Seven Pillars of Wisdom*. *Ashmolean Museum, Oxford*

He had arrived on 16 October. On the 19th he and Storrs embarked for Rabegh, the next port north on the Arabian coast, where he met the Sherif's eldest son, Ali. He got short shrift: 'He is obviously a very conscientious, careful, pleasant, gentleman, without force of character, nervous and rather tired. His physical weakness makes him subject to quick fits of shaking passion with more frequent moods of infirm obstinacy. Apparently not ambitious for himself, but swayed somewhat too easily by the wishes of others...'

Lawrence was now the more eager to meet Feisal, but he was encamped with his small force a hundred miles inland in Wadi Safra, requiring permission, camels and guides to effect a meeting. Ali was not happy at this prospect, but Abdullah had sent a written request in his father's name, so Lawrence got his way. After a strenuous journey with only brief respites, he reached Feisal's headquarters in the village of Hamra on the afternoon of October 23. He and his guides forded a little stream, advanced up a walled path between trees, and brought their camels to the kneel by the yard-gate of a long low house. A slave led Lawrence to an inner court, on whose further side, framed between the uprights of a black doorway, stood a striking white-robed figure. If the arrival in Jidda was the overture, this was the grand opening scene, the meeting of the two principals, the young guru and the slightly older grandee who together would be at the heart of the coming campaign. This is Lawrence's account in *Seven Pillars*:

I felt at first glance that this was the man I had come to Arabia to seek – the leader who would bring the Arab Revolt to full glory. Feisal looked very tall and pillar-like, very slender, in his long white silk robes and his brown head-cloth bound with a brilliant scarlet and gold cord. His eyelids were dropped; and his black beard and colourless face were like a mask against the strange, still watchfulness of his body. His hands were crossed in front of him on his dagger.

I greeted him. He made way for me into the room, and sat down on his carpet near the door. As my eyes grew accustomed to the shade, they saw that the little room held many silent figures, looking at me or at Feisal steadily. He remained staring down at his hands, which were twisting slowly about his dagger. At last he inquired softly how I had found the journey. I spoke of the heat, and he asked how long from Rabegh, commenting that I had ridden fast for the season. 'And do you like our place here in Wadi Safra?' 'Well; but it is far from Damascus.'

In that moment, Lawrence would have us believe, the true agenda of the Arab Revolt was declared: that it should not confine itself to the Arabian desert but strike north to the heartlands of Syria, making the Syrian capital, Damascus, its objective. Only thus would the schemes of the French, and also of the British – for Lawrence was ambivalent about his own country's ambitions – be outwitted and the Arabs achieve what he believed was their destiny and birthright.

At Jidda the heat of Arabia had struck like a drawn sword. Again he used the same potent simile. At the mention of 'Damascus', he wrote: 'The word had fallen like a sword in their midst. There was a quiver. Then everybody present stiffened where he sat, and held his breath for a silent minute. Some, perhaps, were dreaming of far off success: others may have thought it a reflection on their late defeat. Feisal at length lifted his eyes, smiling at me, and said, "Praise be to God, there are Turks nearer us than that".'

It is a powerful moment, but it is important to the understanding of both Lawrence and his book, that it didn't necessarily happen exactly like that. As well as compiling his personal notes, Lawrence was keeping a diary of his journey. Of his first encounter with Feisal he wrote: 'I found him in a little mud house built on a twenty-foot knoll of earth, busied with many visitors. Had a short and rather lively talk, and then excused myself... I had a bath and slept really well, after dining and arguing with Feisal (who was most unreasonable) for hours and hours.'

Of course, strictly there is no reason to suspect that the 'short and lively talk' did not contain the dramatic exchange as described in *Seven Pillars*. But a straight reading of Lawrence's notes might seem to suggest that he found Feisal in a downbeat rather than a positive mood, one in which he might not have been overly responsive to striking gestures by untried strangers. If Feisal was out of sorts he had good reason. He was at Hamra having been driven back by a resurgent Turkish force which had recovered from an earlier setback and threatened to push him even further towards the coast. On the next day the Emir and the ardent young officer had 'another hot discussion' which lasted from 6.30 a.m. till noon. This ended amicably, however, while at a further meeting 'everything went smoothly, and he seemed less nervy. His optimism, or his contempt of the possibility of a Turkish advance, seemed curiously fixed.'

If Lawrence had set himself to draw Feisal out of his negative attitude he had clearly succeeded, and it did not take long for him to give his host a glowing report. Three days after their first encounter, his 'Personal Notes on the Sherifial Family', despatched to Cairo from the coastal port of Yenbo, portray the thirty-one year-old Emir as

'... *tall, graceful, vigorous, almost regal in appearance... Far more imposing personally than any of his brothers, knows it and trades on it. Is as clear-skinned as a pure Circassian, with dark hair, vivid black eyes set a little sloping in his face, strong nose, short chin. Looks like a European, and very like the monument of Richard I, at Fontevraud. He is hot tempered, proud and impatient, sometimes unreasonable, and runs off easily at tangents. Possesses far more personal magnetism and life than his brothers, but less prudence. Obviously very clever, perhaps not over scrupulous. Rather narrow-minded, and rash when he acts on impulse, but usually with enough strength to reflect, and then exact in judgment. Had he been brought up the wrong way might have become a barrack-yard officer. A popular idol, and ambitious; full of dreams, and the capacity to realise them, with keen personal insight, and a very efficient man of business.*

As for the account in his book, whatever the precise realities of their first meeting, retrospectively Lawrence doubtless saw it as a defining moment that called for special emphasis, which is why he might have turned a series of disparate exchanges into a major scene. This was, after all, the finding of the one on whom the election should fall; his likening of Feisal to Richard the Lionheart was the strongest possible endorsement. And there can be little doubt that at the heart of their encounter was a meeting of minds on the vital question as to where the revolt should now go: that it should turn away from its localised obsession with Mecca and Medina and look north, towards Syria and – the necessary goal on the far horizon – Damascus.

He returned to Egypt by a roundabout route. From Jidda he sailed in HMS *Euryalus* to Port Sudan, en route for Khartoum, where he met Sir Reginald Wingate, the Commander-in-Chief of the Egyptian Army, who was responsible for the Hejaz operations. Back in Cairo he joined the newly formed Arab Bureau – created to act as a Staff and Intelligence Office for the Arabian campaign. It was a time of intense activity and argument, as the Allies and the Arabs sought the best way to advance the Grand Sherif's campaign. To this end, Wingate decided that British support for the Arabs required better communi-cation between Cairo and the Hejaz, an early step being his order that Lawrence should return – initially for two weeks – to undertake liaison duties with Feisal.

This decision was hardly consistent with the immediate impressions aroused among certain other senior officers during Lawrence's first visit to Arabia. Thus Colonel Wilson described him, in a letter to Brigadier-General Clayton in Cairo, as a 'bumptious young ass who spoils his undoubted knowledge of Syrian Arabs etc. by making himself out to be the only authority on war, engineering, running H.M's ships and everything else. He put every single person's back up I've met, from the Admiral down to the most junior fellow on the Red Sea.' Captain Boyle of HMS *Euryalus* would confess himself 'a little astonished when a small, untidily dressed and most unmilitary figure strolled up to me on board the ship I was temporarily commanding and said, hands in pockets and so without a salute: "I'm going over to Port Sudan"'. Colonel Pierce Joyce, a regular officer of the Connaught Rangers, who met him on his arrival at Port Sudan, would later own to 'an intense desire on my part to tell him to get his hair cut and that his uniform and dirty buttons badly needed the attention of his batman'.

Opposite: Lawrence as the world would
come to see him. Though many of his
later desert journeys were by armoured
car, it was as a hard-riding cameleer
that he first impressed the Arab
tribesmen and as he would always
remain in the popular imagination.
Imperial War Museum, Q 601212

All this would now change. On his return to Feisal's headquarters Lawrence
quickly re-established their relationship and Feisal asked him to stay on as his
adviser. The Emir also suggested that Lawrence should wear Arab clothes,
concerned that if he were to be much about the camp it would be better if he
did not stand out in khaki uniform but merged into the general scene. Lawrence
accepted with alacrity, aware that this would give him greater presence, and – a
matter too easily ignored – at necessary personal moments a greater privacy, his
view being (as quoted earlier) that in the desert Arab clothes were 'cleaner and
more decent', as compared to the clumsy jacket and trousers of Western dress,
whether military or civilian. So the untidy young subaltern who had irritated
so many of his compatriots emerged as a figure of style and authority in Feisal's
entourage, and began the process of becoming the recognizable figure of legend.

Colonel Joyce, whose eyebrows had risen in annoyance at the first sight
of him, would shortly see the new Lawrence in action at an important meeting
of Arab leaders, Lawrence being by this time closely involved in the strategic
decisions of the campaign:

*On this occasion his appearance was such a contrast to the untidy Lieutenant I had met
at Port Sudan that one suddenly became aware of contact with a very unusual personality.
He was beautifully robed in a black abba with a deep gold border; a guftan [i.e. kaftan]
of finest white Damascus silk with wide flowing sleeves, bound at the waist with a belt
containing a large curved gold dagger; a kofia or headcloth of rich embroidered silk, kept in
place by an agal [headrope] of white and gold; sandals on his bare feet – in every detail a
truly distinguished picturesque figure indistinguishable from any of the nobles of the royal
house of Hussein seated round us.*

Wadi Rumm, for Lawrence more than a merely dramatic phenomenon of the Arabian desert, rather a place of moral and philosophical significance. He wrote in *Seven Pillars*: 'Later, when we were often riding inland my mind used to turn me from the direct road to clear my senses by a night in Rumm...
I would say, "Shall I ride on this time, beyond the Khazail, and know it all?" '.
Author photograph

Lawrence himself described his transformation somewhat more jauntily, in a letter to Major Kinahan Cornwallis, Director of the Arab Bureau, in the last days of 1916: 'I want to rub off my British habits and go off with Feisal for a bit. Amusing job and all new country.'

'All new country': yet in this far country Lawrence had now definitely found his true terrain. Deserts have long stimulated the Anglo-Saxon imagination, whether the cold deserts of the Polar regions, or the hot deserts of Africa, Asia or the Middle East. Chapter I of the Introduction to *Seven Pillars of Wisdom* strikes the appropriate note in its very first sentences: 'Some of the evil of my tale may have been inherent in our circumstances. For years we lived anyhow with one another in the naked desert, under the indifferent heaven. By day the hot sun fermented us; and we were dizzied by the beating wind. At night we were stained by dew, and shamed into pettiness by the innumerable silences of stars.'

This was a man fascinated and inspired by the landscape he fought in. Not a few officers carried cameras with them during the campaign, but Lawrence was unusual in that many of his photographs are of scenes with minimal human or animal content and, arguably, with little or no strategic value or justification. They are desert abstracts, hills and crags and valleys framed to show them as aspects of nature, patterns and

shapes thrown up by the processes of creation, the photographer clearly relishing their austere and rarely seen beauty. It is almost as though no one had noticed or been moved by such landscapes before so they had to be scrupulously recorded.

Yet some subjects he seems to have seen as beyond the perception of his camera, chief among them that hundred-mile-long masterpiece of nature – almost a kind of Grand Canyon of the desert – Wadi Rumm. Here he resorted to the mental photography of fine words, describing it, in obvious awe, as 'this irresistible place: this processional way greater than imagination'. Of his first visit there, he wrote: 'Our little caravan grew self-conscious and fell dead quiet, afraid and ashamed to flaunt its smallness in the presence of the stupendous hills. Landscapes, in childhood's dream, were so vast and silent.' It was a place he would often return to for spiritual refreshment and which he would never forget.

The desert, however, was not just the setting, the background to the unusual campaign to which Lawrence was committed; it was also an essential weapon. The Arabs were fighting a conventionally trained enemy, with infantry and artillery and standard logistical support. In head-to-head encounters they would have no chance: indeed if they were drawn into such a situation they resorted to a simple solution; they turned and fled. Lawrence articulated the only possible response. The Arabs would have little hope of success, he argued, if they came like an army with banners:

… but suppose we were (as we might be) an influence, an idea, a thing intangible, invulnerable, without front or back, drifting about like a gas? Armies were like plants, immobile, firm-rooted, nourished through long stems to the head. We might be a vapour, blowing where we listed…

Most wars were wars of contact, both forces striving into touch to avoid tactical surface. Ours should be a war of detachment. We were to contain the enemy by the silent threat of a vast, unknown desert...

If the Arabs struck their attack should be largely 'nominal', directed not against the enemy in person but against 'his stuff... his most accessible material':

In railway-cutting it would usually be an empty stretch of rail; and the more empty, the greater the tactical success. We might turn our average into a rule... and develop a habit of never engaging the enemy... Our cue was to destroy, not the Turk's army, but his minerals. The death of a Turkish bridge or rail, machine or gun or charge of high explosive, was more profitable to us than the death of a Turk.

In this Lawrence was articulating if not a protest against, at least a dissension from, the attitude to losses prevalent in all the belligerent countries throughout the 1914–18 war: 'Governments saw men only in mass; but our men, being irregulars, were not formations, but individuals. An individual death, like a pebble dropped in water, might make but a brief hole; yet rings of sorrow widened out therefrom. We could not afford casualties.'

'Rings of sorrow': it is a potent phrase, and a prophetic one. Who can deny but that the rings of sorrow from that uniquely dreadful war ripple on to this day?

These sentences, which appear in a key chapter in *Seven Pillars*, number XXXIII in Book III, are from another of Lawrence's set-piece passages. In March 1917, when visiting the camp of Emir Abdullah in Wadi Ais, he was taken ill, and lay ten days in his tent, taking advantage of his forced inaction to think through the strategy and tactics of the campaign. His conclusions form a ten-page thesis in the book, a sustained diatribe, that could almost be reprinted straight as a military monograph. This has led to claims that he did not elaborate his ideas at

Opposite: Lawrence at Damascus,
portrait by the official war artist,
James McBey. Painted on 3 October,
1918 (the day before his return to
Europe), it captured a Lawrence who
was physically drained and, to quote
his own expression, whose 'main
springs of action [were] exhausted'.
Imperial War Museum Department of Art

the time, but compiled them afterwards for effect and with the advantage of hindsight. Such claims are clearly disproved by one of his earliest despatches, a document entitled 'Military Notes' written in Jidda back in November 1916, in which he had emphasized that the real sphere of the tribes was guerrilla warfare, that the Arabs were too individualistic to endure commands or fight in line, so that it would be impossible to make an organized force out of them, but that they could dynamite a railway, plunder a caravan, steal camels. He had also added this, in a forceful codicil arguing against the idea of landing foreign, particularly Christian, troops in the desert:

The Hejaz war is one of dervishes against regular troops — and we are on the side of the dervishes. Our text-books do not apply to its conditions at all. It is the fight of a rocky, mountainous, ill-watered country (assisted by a wild horde of mountaineers) against a force which has been improved — so far as civilised warfare is concerned — so immensely by the Germans, as almost to have lost its efficiency for rough-and-tumble work.

These thoughts were on their way to Headquarters in Cairo just nineteen days after Lawrence landed in Arabia and under a fortnight after his first meeting with Feisal. They were duly published in the newly launched *Arab Bulletin*, which, containing the best of the intelligence summaries submitted to the Arab Bureau, was to develop into a publication of considerable distinction. Edited for much of its run with an insistence on clarity and good style by Lawrence's former mentor, D.G. Hogarth — now an officer in the Royal Navy — it had a restricted but high-level readership, even reaching the desk in London of the Chief of the Imperial General Staff, Sir William Robertson. Few officers of junior rank had their reports and activities commented on by the Empire's leading soldier, but Captain T.E. Lawrence was one of them. He had established himself very clearly as a man to watch.

5

'It is of course by far the most
wonderful time I have had'.

The desert war: the action and the fulfilment

The Arab Revolt had no future unless it moved north. There was no virtue in staying in the vicinity of Medina where it had begun, pecking at the Turkish garrison holed up there and the Turkish forces in its vicinity. By moving north the Revolt would widen its appeal, bring in more tribes and expose more of the Hejaz Railway (the umbilical cord between Damascus and Arabia on which Lawrence had once travelled as a peaceful passenger) to the kind of harassment of which he knew the Arabs were supremely capable. He soon became a practitioner in the art of sabotage himself, and certainly at first relished the tip-and-run excitement of it. In a letter later that year to Colonel Wilson – who by now had conceded that the eccentric new arrival had more to him than mere bumptiousness – Lawrence praised his superior officer for his supportive staff-work in Jidda, adding that 'if ever I can get my book out' he would try to make people see how vital such work was. 'They don't seem always to appreciate that while we hop about the Railway and places smashing things up, and enjoying ourselves, someone else has to sit in Jidda keeping the head of the affair on the rails.'

Two things are evident from the above; his satisfaction of having participated in the active side of his war, and the fact that he made no secret of his ambition ultimately to turn his experiences into a book.

Initially, it might have seemed that any book he wrote would emerge as an upbeat adventure story, as, in the phrase of the time, ' a ripping yarn'. That key word was not far from his mind when, writing to Captain Newcombe (formerly of the Sinai expedition, now himself involved in the desert campaign), he described Feisal as 'an absolute ripper', while when sending a few photographs to his family – to 'give you an idea of the sort of country and the sort of people we have to do with' – he added in his accompanying letter: 'It is of course by far the most wonderful time I have had'.

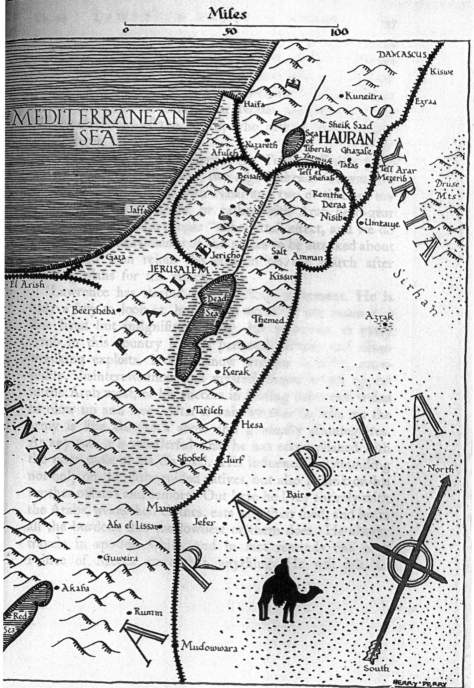

THE CAMPAIGN IN THE NORTH

Miles

0   50   100

MEDITERRANEAN SEA

DAMASCUS
Kiswe
Kuneitra
Ezra
Haifa
Sheik Saad
Sea of Tiberias   HAURAN
Nazareth   Ghazale
Afuleh   R. Yarmuk   Tafas
Beisan   Tell Arar
Tell et sheñab   Mezerib
Druse Mts
Remthe
Jaff   Deraa
Nisib
Umtaiye
Jericho   Salt   Amman
JERUSALEM   Kissir
Gaza
El Arish   Dead Sea   Sirhan
Beersheba   Themed   Azrak
Kerak
Tafileh   Hesa
North
Shobek   Jurf
Bair
Maan
Afa el Lissan   Jefer
Guweira
Akaba   Rumm
South
Red Sea   Mudowwara

HERRY PERRY

Previous page: The territory of the later
stages of the Arab campaign, from
Akaba to Damascus. Other key places
featured include (south to north):
Rumm, Maan, Tafileh, Azrak, Amman,
Deraa, Tafas, the River Yarmuk; also,
to the west of the Jordan, Jerusalem,
Jaffa, Nazareth, Haifa. Map by Herry
Perry from *Lawrence and the Arabs*, by
Robert Graves, 1927.
Courtesy of Carcanet Press Ltd

If there had been any doubts in Cairo about his being assigned to the desert
they were soon discarded. 'The value of Lawrence in the position which he has
made for himself with Feisul [sic] is enormous,' wrote Brigadier-General Clayton
to a fellow officer in March 1917. Significantly, writing in April, Lawrence himself
stated tellingly that at Feisal's headquarters 'one lives in a continual atmosphere
of effort and high thinking towards a better conduct of the war'. This was the
powerhouse of the Revolt and Lawrence was at the heart of it.

It was about this time that Colonel Joyce, who like Wilson had revised his
original opinion, saw Lawrence in conference with a group of senior Arabs and
noted his deft, unassuming techniques of persuasion.

At this as at dozens of other conferences we attended together Lawrence rarely spoke. He
merely studied the men around him and when the arguments ended, as they usually did,
in smoke, he then dictated his plan of action which was usually adopted and everybody
went away satisfied. It was not as is often supposed by his individual leadership of hordes
of Bedouins that he achieved successes in his daring ventures, but by a wise selection of
tribal leaders and by providing the essential grist to the mill in the shape of golden rewards
for work well done.

Joyce's final words emphasize a vital aspect of the Revolt; if some of the more
far-sighted Arabs were fighting for a cause, the mass of ordinary fighters were
fighting for cash. Lawrence had been well aware of this from the beginning, but
he was also confident that once on the salary-roll they would stay loyal. In his
already quoted 'Military Notes' of the previous November he had stated: 'It is
customary to sneer at their love of pay, but it is notable that in spite of bribes, the
Hejaz tribes are not helping the Turks, and that the Sherif's supply columns are
everywhere going without escort in perfect safety'.

The Arab Army on the march, with the Emir Feisal pictured centre. In this action photograph by Lawrence, January 1917, his closeness to the Emir clearly indicates his privileged status.
Imperial War Museum Q58863

There was another reason for optimism. The tribes had suspended their blood feuds for the period of the war, and would fight side by side, 'if they have a Sherif [i.e. a descendent of the Prophet] in supreme command'. Since Hussein and his four sons were Sherifs, the prospects were good, though they would be better if the Revolt could show signs of actual success.

Success required action, a breakout into new territory. It came early in 1917 with a dramatic move north from Yenbo to Wejh – a significant advance up the Red Sea coast. The occasion provided another of Lawrence's keynote scenes:

Our start was set for January the eighteenth just after noon… We watched Feisal. He got up from his rug, … caught the saddle-pommels in his hands, put his knee on the side… The slave released the camel, which sprang up. When it was on its feet Feisal passed his other leg across its back, swept his skirts and his cloak under him by a wave of the arm, and settled himself in the saddle. As his camel moved we had jumped for ours, and the whole mob rose together, some of the beasts roaring, but the most quiet, as trained she-camels should be… The camels took their first abrupt steps.

He also managed to catch the event with his camera. He developed a definite skill for photographing the Arab Revolt on the march, at a time when his more professional counterparts in France and Flanders were producing classic images of the Western Front conflict, though almost always from static positions and on glass plates. His hand-held Kodak, using 120 negative film, was much more flexible; a contrast which, as it happened, reflected the two differing styles of warfare; the attritional log-jam in France, the kaleidoscopic, mobile campaign in Arabia.

Wejh was Turkish held, a target to be taken. The agreed strategy was a pincer attack in collaboration with the Royal Navy. He reported to Cairo: 'The manoeuvre was only made possible at all by the absolute command of the sea and the ungrudging co-operation in transport of ammunition and supplies afforded Feisal by the S.N.O. [Senior Naval Officer] Red Sea Patrol.' The naval officer so praised was Captain Boyle, once in command of HMS *Euryalus*, now of HMS *Suva*.

In the event, Feisal was two days behind the agreed schedule and Boyle, fearing the Turkish garrison would decamp, launched his seaborne attacks without waiting for him. Lawrence arrived to find that there had been fierce fighting and some twenty Arab fatalities, while a British lieutenant of the Air Service had been mortally wounded in a seaplane reconnaissance. Though he applauded the success, he was grieved at the cost, believing that with better management even such modest losses might have been avoided. The tiny garrison would have surrendered anyway, he felt, if left to cool its heels for a few days. Indeed, had they all escaped, 'it would not have mattered the value of an Arab life. We wanted Wejh as a base against the railway and to extend our front; the smashing and killing in it had been wanton.'

Looked at with hindsight and in the context of the wider war Lawrence's objections can seem like a lone voice against a tempest. 'Smashing and killing' would become the hallmark of the year just begun; indeed 1917 has been well described as essentially a year of slaughter. As would later be forcefully argued by a Western Front soldier who was to become Lawrence's bitterest critic, Richard Aldington, old-style heroism was out of fashion in the kind of warfare now endemic in Europe; his book *Death of a Hero* would become the classic denunciation of the ancient hero myth. Yet Lawrence's utterly different war needed its charismatic figureheads and he was shortly to find one, who, apart from a few moments of disfavour and an undeniable lust for gold, was to fight with him valiantly to the end.

Auda Abu Tayi, veteran chief of the Howeitat tribe, appears in the story like an approaching champion, his stature and reputation indicated by his being described as an 'immense chivalrous name'. It is almost as if a Galahad is on his way to lead the search for the Grail; indeed, it is no surprise to find the term 'knight-errant' attached to him. The moment when he steps on to the stage, or, more precisely, enters Feisal's tent, is inevitably one of high drama:

I was about to take my leave when Suleiman, the guest-master, hurried in and whispered to Feisal, who turned to me with shining eyes, trying to be calm, and said 'Auda is here'. I shouted 'Auda abu Tayi', and at that moment the tent-flap was drawn back… There entered a tall, strong figure, with a haggard face, passionate and tragic… He might be over fifty, and his black hair was streaked with white; but he was still strong and straight, loosely built, spare, and as active as a much younger man. His face was magnificent in its lines and hollows.

Lawrence's description of Auda in *Seven Pillars* is no richer than that he wrote for the *Arab Bulletin* in July 1917. Thus:

He sees life as a saga. All events in it are significant and all personages heroic. His mind is packed (and generally overflows) with stories of old raids and epic poems of fights. When he cannot secure a listener he sings to himself in his tremendous voice, which is also deep and musical. In the echoing valleys of Arnousa, our guide in night marches was this wonderful voice of Auda's, conversing far in the van, and being rolled back to us from the broken faces of the cliffs.

Auda's intervention was due to his strong feeling that the Revolt should keep on moving north; he arrived, wrote Lawrence, 'chafing at our delay in Wejh'. Out of this combustible combination, Auda's martial ardour, Feisal's vision and political determination, and Lawrence's eye for strategic advantage, there was now to emerge the most daring move of the whole Revolt.

The seizure of the port of Akaba, at the north-eastern end of the Red Sea, from the landward side, was in many ways the campaign's make-or-break moment. The generally accepted wisdom was that it should be attacked head-on from the sea. The British and French saw it as the next obvious target. As if to

The veteran leader of the Howeitat tribe, Auda abu Tayi in a post-war photograph. Lawrence wrote of him: 'His face was magnificent in its lines and hollows. He had large eloquent eyes, like black velvet in richness. His forehead was low and broad, his nose very high and sharp, powerfully hooked.' Some wartime photographs do Auda less than justice, he having smashed his false teeth, because they were Turkish.
Bodleian Library

confirm this, Akaba's guns faced seaward in anticipation. But Lawrence coveted Akaba for the Arabs, who could never take it by frontal assault but might do so if they mounted a surprise attack from inland. Whose idea it was to implement this daring strategy has been much debated, the distinguished Jordanian historian Suleiman Mousa claiming it an Arab initiative. Yet however arrived at, the concept is well in line with Lawrence's philosophy as evolved in his ten days of fever in Abdullah's camp. They would bear down on Akaba 'like a gas', appearing unexpectedly out of 'the vast, unknown desert'.

But there were other aspects to this scheme. Akaba was not just a trophy to be won in order to cut a dash and assert Arab pride. Beyond Akaba lay the road north to the key railway junction at Maan, the only route by which the Arab forces could strike towards Syria and so become involved in the major Allied campaign against the Turks, to which it was important that the Arab effort should be indissolubly joined. For this was where the outcome of the Middle Eastern campaign would be decided, and it was vital that the Revolt should make a significant contribution to that decision.

On 9 May, 1917, a small expedition of about fifty men, carrying 20,000 gold sovereigns and a mass of explosive, left Wejh, heading out into the desert on a wide loop, with a view to arriving secretly at a point of vantage from which Akaba might be attacked. The force was commanded by another of Lawrence's heroes, Sherif Nasir, whom he would later praise, in recognition of his sustained contribution to the cause as 'the opener of roads, the forerunner of Feisal's movement, the man who fired his first shot in Medina, and who was to fire our last shot at Muslimieh beyond Aleppo on the day that Turkey asked for an armistice', concluding: 'From beginning to end all that could be told of him was good.'

This was not, however, to be a breezy desert jaunt, a ripping adventure without shadow. From the start Lawrence knew he was acting without official sanction. Had he tried to clear his scheme with Cairo, he might not have won the required approval. So: 'I decided to go my own way, with or without orders. I wrote a letter full of apologies to Clayton, telling him that my intentions were of the best: and went.'

But there was a second, greater burden than that of mere insubordination. He had known for some time of the so-called Sykes-Picot agreement, an Anglo-French understanding about the post-war division of the Middle East arrived at with scant concern for Arab hopes and ambitions. The Akaba expedition, indeed the whole progress of the Revolt, depended on raising serious support among the tribes, on persuading men to quit their tents to face wounds or death, but with the distinct possibility that those who survived might return, if they were so lucky, with a minimal bag of gold and having gained no political advantage. Yet he also knew that if the Arabs could prove their military worth they would

'I decided to go my own way, with or without orders. I wrote a letter full of apologies to Clayton, telling him that my intentions were of the best: and went.'

greatly improve their chances of political reward. By contrast, if they did nothing, nothing would be achieved. The cause must be pursued with full vigour, and if it were necessary – since total frankness on this subject could be fatal to any tribal enthusiasm – there would have to be 'cover-up', prevarication, deliberate avoidance of the truth. At all costs, even the cost of his own sense of integrity and honour, the Arab tribal leaders had to be kept on side.

As if this were not enough, the going proved excessively hard. Four days into the march Lawrence caught a high fever and was troubled by boils. 'Pain and agony today', he wrote in his little notebook diary on 13 May. Conditions worsened, with difficult ground, a wind like a furnace, dust getting everywhere, dryness in the throat, though there was some relief in the salt sweat-drops that dripped like ice-water from his hair. On the 24th, crossing an area of dried mud flats called the Biseita, it was realised one of the party was missing, presumably having fallen off his camel when asleep. Lawrence turned back to search for him, finding the man, Gasim, almost maddened by the sun. They regained the expedition, but Sherif Nasir was furious with Lawrence's servants, Ali and Othman, for letting him go back alone, and beat them. Lawrence seems to have been too exhausted to intervene. 'Not their fault', he noted. 'I didn't tell. Think tonight worst yet of my experience.'

At last they reached the kindlier terrain of the Wadi Sirhan, with its occasional wells and vegetation. This was Auda's country, the home of the Howeitat tribe; from here he had gone south to pledge his support to Feisal, now he had the chance to show he could deliver what he had promised. While Auda rallied his people Nasir and Lawrence moved from place to place enlisting. There was much din and excitement, with giving of gifts and firing of rifles. There were also numerous tribal feasts, for which Lawrence had no appetite. 'Have feasted

Lawrence's unsent signal to Clayton,
June 1916; crossed out but still just
legible. This message, written on the
eve of his controversial northern
journey during the Akaba expedition,
surely represents the lowest point of
Lawrence's war.
The British Library, Add. MS 45915, f.55v

noon and sunset since evening of May 27,' he noted, 'and am very tired of it';
but he also commented that he had been 'twenty-eight years well fed and had no
right to despise these fellows for loving their mutton.' Worst of all was the ordeal
of having to answer questions from would-be recruits as to future prospects and
Allied intentions. On 2 June he wrote: 'All day deputations, fusillades, coffee,
ostrich eggs. Dined with Auda. Lies.'

There followed one of the strangest episodes of Lawrence's wartime career.
On 5 June he wrote: 'Can't stand another day here. Will ride north and chuck
it.' This in the personal diary; in a signals' book he scribbled a message which he
later tried to cross out but which nevertheless remained decipherable: 'Clayton.
I've decided to go off alone to Damascus, hoping to get killed on the way: for all

sakes try and clear this show up before it goes further. We are calling them to fight for us on a lie, and I can't stand it.'

He left Nasir's camp and rode off in a mood of deep despair. Yet, curiously, what began with a virtual suicide note ended a month later with a secret report written in Cairo providing incisive information about the northern tribes which gave every impression of being a rigorous professional assessment by an intelligence operative in complete control. This was how he was able to present his impulsive excursion to the world, but it was not how it was conceived or begun, as he admitted in a version of *Seven Pillars* (the so-called Oxford text of 1922), in which he described his journey as 'long and dangerous, no part of the machinery of the revolt, as barren of consequence as it was unworthy in motive'. Yet he could genuinely, or so it seems, find a justification for the episode in that it had given him a chance to update his knowledge of Syria and 'put straight the ideas of strategic geography given me by the Crusades and the first Arab conquest'. A resourceful officer taking advantage of a lull in the action to bone up professionally for the next phase of the campaign? A man of deep religious background battling with a profound sense of shame? In Lawrence both these personae rode together through the fearsome desert heat.

He returned to Nasir's camp to find the slow process of recruitment over at last and the assembled force ready to move towards Akaba. Early July saw a brief surprise attack on a Turkish battalion barring their route at Abu el Lissan, with withering sniper fire costing many Turkish lives and producing a large crop of prisoners, and Lawrence adding a bizarre twist to the encounter by clumsily shooting his own camel in the head during the charge.

The slaughter of 400 Turks produced in him an extraordinary reaction given that no campaign, however surgically fought, could avoid its crop of fatalities.

That night he went out to muse over the fallen enemy. 'The dead men looked wonderfully beautiful. The night was shining gently down, softening them into new ivory... [However,] the corpses seemed flung so pitifully on the ground, huddled anyhow in low heaps. Surely if straightened they would be comfortable at last. So I put them all in order, one by one.' Lawrence had just returned from a wild excursion in which he had by his own admission deliberately offered up his person to be killed. It was as if, by adjusting the Turkish bodies he was virtually tending his own.

On the 6th the expedition reached its goal. It was a climactic moment: 'We raced through a driving sand-storm down to Akaba, ... and splashed into the sea.' But there was no fiercely resisting garrison to overcome, no casualty toll to deplore as at Wejh. In the moment of success Lawrence shot, not his camel, but a remarkable action picture of the final charge.

His report for the *Arab Bulletin* on the occupation of Akaba was markedly matter-of-fact. He was not out to wave flags. He noted the 'comic' astonishment of a German N.C.O., at Akaba to bore for wells, who 'knew neither Arabic, nor Turkish, and had not been aware of the Arab revolt.' He pointed out that Akaba's situation was 'now rather serious, economically', with little food, 600 prisoners and many visitors in prospect. He emphasised the port's potential as a base by indicating that tribal elements were already scouting to the north and south, with a view to opening up the next phase of the Arabian campaign.

The Arab force was in desperate need of supplies, so Lawrence left immediately for Cairo arriving there on 10 July. Eight days earlier, on 2 July, Brigadier-General Clayton had written: 'It is not known what are the present whereabouts of Captain Lawrence, who left for the Maan area or Jebel Druse area some time ago.' Suddenly he was there, walking into Clayton's office and

The charge into Akaba, 6 July 1916; action photograph by T.E. Lawrence. The capture of Akaba – 'for months... the horizon of our mind, the goal' – was the turning-point of the Arab Revolt. *Imperial War Museum Q 59193*

with Akaba in his pocket. If he feared that his disregard for orders would produce a stern rebuke he need not have worried. In his absence the Egyptian Expeditionary Force – Britain's principal force in the Middle East – had mounted an attack against Turkish positions at Gaza. It had failed in an earlier offensive and now it had failed again. 1917 was a year with few gains to celebrate and lack of success in any theatre was not readily indulged. The Commander-in-Chief of the Middle Eastern Expeditionary Force, General Sir Archibald Murray, had been sent back home, and a new C-in-C, General Sir Edmund Allenby, had replaced him. Cairo could now greet Allenby with unexpected good news. For Lawrence was not alone in recognising that by seizing Akaba the Arab Revolt was

Opposite: Sir Edmund Allenby, always
known to his soldiers as 'The Bull':
portrait in pastel by Eric Kennington,
1921. Lawrence once wrote of it:
'As a portrait of Allenby the drawing
is unusually rich, and Allenby is an
admiration of mine.'
National Portrait Gallery

no longer out of sight over the southern horizon. It was a factor which the new
supremo might use to advantage.

Before long the two were brought together: the big bemedalled cavalry
general fresh from France – whose physical impact can be gauged by his
nickname 'The Bull' – and Lawrence, who self-deprecatingly dubbed himself 'a
little bare-footed silk-skirted man offering to hobble the enemy by his preaching
if given stores and arms and a fund of two hundred thousand sovereigns to
convince and control his converts'. These two quite different personalities sized
each other up and immediately saw that they could collaborate to their mutual
benefit. It was as if for once David and Goliath were on the same side. Allenby
perceived Lawrence's worth and Lawrence recognised a man he could work with.
For Allenby, who had come from a brutal, impersonal style of war from which
he himself had been effectively sacked for inadequate achievement, saw this as a
campaign where different rules applied and where he could thrive. The soldier-
historian Cyril Falls later wrote of him, approvingly: 'He restored the old personal
relationship between leader and troops which was one of the finest traditions
of the British Army in the past and one of the keys to its successes. He was
constantly up and down the line, so that there can have been few commanders in
modern warfare who were so well known to their troops.' He was thus precisely
the kind of commander whom Lawrence craved; he was 'the nearest to my
longings for a master'.

There have been numerous attempts to assert that Lawrence won his fame
only by self-aggrandisement, that he was a minor player who retrospectively
claimed, or allowed others to claim for him, a far greater role than he deserved.
The supreme justification for Lawrence is the fact that Allenby, who effectively
won the Middle Eastern war, believed in him and made use of what he had to

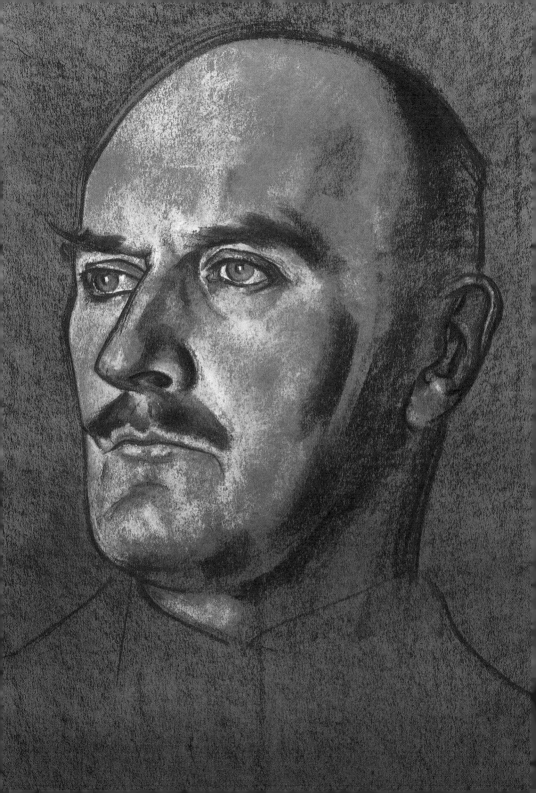

offer. This was no sentimental attachment to a maverick with extravagant notions. It was a recognition that there was military advantage in what Feisal's guerrilla force could achieve, with Lawrence at the Emir's side to pass on and interpret the behests of Cairo and in particular of the new Commander-in-Chief. Allenby's mission was to defeat the Turks in regular warfare. The Arabs could help with their irregular tactics in a number of ways. They could cut signals and goods traffic on the Hejaz railway; damage or destroy trucks and locomotives which the enemy would find it hard if not impossible to replace; act as a shield and as an intelligence force on Allenby's right flank, their very presence ensuring that the Turks could not concentrate their forces against their principal opponents as they would have wished. Akaba was to prove a useful base for these activities, though necessarily the lines of communication grew longer as the focus of the campaign moved steadily north.

A new energy entered Lawrence's attitude at this time. Supported by Allenby the conventional soldier, Lawrence and his unconventional tactics were able to claim ever greater success, with his taunting of the Turks, his forays behind Turkish lines, and his sudden descents on the railway. Colonel Joyce noted the change, and the fact that his highly individual style seemed to produce a creative response in his Arab allies:

His individual bravery and endurance captured their imagination. Initial successes made 'Auruns', as the Arabs called him, a byword in the desert and there was always competition among the sheikhs to ride with him on a foray. Like the rest of us he had many disappointments but nothing could shake his determination to win through or his restless energy in initiating alternative plans when things went wrong and the whole scheme had to be re-cast...

It was an astonishing transformation. Now the Oxford archaeologist-cum-soldier was much to be seen in the company of a mass of hawk-eyed cameleers specially recruited as his escort, ready to go where he wished to go and fight where he fought. He took the situation almost lightly, impressed as much by the look of them as by their potential in action. 'My bodyguard of fifty Arab tribesmen,' he wrote, 'are more splendid than a tulip garden.'

Increasingly breezy reports came in from Lawrence in the desert describing the campaign's progress. Yet he was ever two persons rather than one: the ardent achiever, the agoniser racked by self-doubt. After the Harret Ammar railway-raid in September, a particularly bloody affair with many enemy casualties, he wrote two letters in quite different moods on successive days. Thus on 24 September to E.T. Leeds:

I'm not going to last out this game much longer: nerves going and temper wearing thin, and one wants an unlimited amount of both…

I hope when the nightmare ends that I will wake up and become alive again. This killing and killing of Turks is horrible. When you charge in at the finish and find them all over the place in bits, and still alive, many of them, and know that you have done hundreds in the same way before and must do hundreds more if you can…

Yet on the following day, in a letter to Major Frank Stirling, a regular army officer who was about to join the Arab campaign as a General Staff Officer, he described the 'stunt' – as he called it – at considerable length, concluding:

The whole job took ten minutes, and they lost 70 killed, 30 wounded, 80 prisoners, and about 25 got away. Of my hundred Howeitat and two British NCOs, there was one (Arab) killed, and four (Arabs) wounded.

The Turks then nearly cut us off as we looted the train, and I lost some baggage, and nearly myself. My loot is a superfine red Baluch prayer-rug.

I hope this sounds the fun it is. The only pity is the sweat to work them up, and the wild scramble while it lasts. It's the most amateurish, Buffalo Billy sort of performance, and the only people who do it well are the Bedouin.

If Lawrence's story were a fiction, or a drama, the next set-piece would have to be the punishment scene. After the successes, the glowing reports, the gongs, the promotion – he was now a major and had been awarded the C.B. (that prestigious, peculiarly British award known as the Companionship of the Bath) – there would be the inevitable chastisement of hubris. Too much pride would require a fall; the hero would have to be captured and put to the rack. It duly happened, the more deservedly because in early November a raid mounted at Allenby's personal request, with the aim of destroying a key railway bridge in the Yarmuk Valley, on the line linking Palestine with the Hejaz Railway, ended in humiliating failure. As the party of sixty Arab guerrillas armed with fifteen sacks of dynamite approached the bridge one man dropped his rifle, a Turkish guard heard the sound and the would-be raiders fled in a hail of bullets. They withdrew to the sanctuary of the old castle at Azrak, east of the future Jordanian capital, Amman, but Lawrence could not rest. He decided, in disguise, to carry out a nocturnal reconnaissance of the key railway junction at Deraa, where in more peaceable times he had once enjoyed a pleasant buffet lunch. But this was no sleepy desert settlement manned by a token handful of soldiers; rather it was a teeming garrison-town. In brief, he was caught, brutally flogged, and, so it would seem, subjected to male rape. He claimed his arch-tormentor to be the Bey of Deraa. Whether this was the case or not, he was given more sophisticatedly savage

'There was no glory left,' he wrote,
'but the terror of the broken flesh,
which had been our own men, carried
past us to their homes.'

treatment than he would have received from a bunch of Turkish N.C.O.s, and in, apparently, the surroundings to match. Whether he was recognized or not is unclear. Somehow before dawn he was either let go or he contrived to escape.

There are those who have doubted whether this episode ever occurred, decrying it as nothing more than a literary concoction. But the signs are too strong to allow so feeble an explanation. 'That night', in which, as he later described it in a moving letter to one of his closest correspondents, Mrs George Bernard Shaw, 'I gave away the only possession we are born into the world with – our bodily integrity', would affect him ever after. It also released in a man with little or no sexual experience – as he put it in the Oxford edition of *Seven Pillars* – something which would 'journey' with him ever after, 'a fascination and terror and morbid desire, lascivious and vicious perhaps, but like the striving of a moth towards its flame.'

Three weeks later he was in a very different situation, worlds away from Yarmuk and Azrak and the dark night of Deraa. The Allies had seized Jerusalem and Lawrence took part in the subsequent triumphal entry. A newsreel film of the time caught him in the crowd as the representatives of the various nations present mingled and chatted after the event; a diminutive figure in conversation with another officer, oddly inconspicuous in borrowed uniform. For a man of his background, however, with his Christian upbringing and his scholarly passion for the Crusades, this was far more than, as it might be thought, an agreeable half-holiday from campaigning; he would describe the ceremony of surrender at the city's Jaffa Gate as, for him, 'the supreme moment of the war'.

Yet, despite that accolade, Jerusalem was only a stage on a more important road, that lead to Damascus. This was still his goal, as it had been from his first meeting with Feisal at Hamra, fourteen hectic months before.

The prospects for the new year, 1918, seemed good, but for Lawrence there were the usual troughs and only occasional triumphs. He achieved one of the latter in a small conventional clash with Turkish forces at Tafileh, to the south of the Dead Sea, in January. A headlong Turkish attack produced 400 Turkish dead and 250 prisoners, the Arab casualties being 25 dead and 40 wounded. Saluted in the Official History of the war as 'a brilliant feat of arms', it did not satisfy Lawrence who felt it could have been avoided and who saw only horror in the aftermath. 'There was no glory left,' he wrote, 'but the terror of the broken flesh, which had been our own men, carried past us to their homes.' His report on the action delighted Headquarters, which 'to crown the jest, offered me a decoration on the strength of it'. He commented, wryly: 'We should have more bright breasts in the Army if each man was able without witnesses, to write out his own despatch.'

February was a bad month, with persistent snow and rain, and bitterly cold. He explained in a letter home: 'The coast and the Dead Sea are warm, but our work lies on the plateau, 4,000 or 5,000 feet up.' Worse, however, were his growing political anxieties. A new hazard had arisen with the so-called 'Balfour Declaration' of November 1917, announcing that the British Government viewed with favour the establishment of a Jewish national home in Palestine, provided the rights of people already living there (mostly Arabs) were not infringed – a virtually impossible equation, as later history would show. Lawrence was asked to ensure that the new development should not affect the Arabs' commitment to the campaign. He wrote to Clayton: 'For the Jews, when I see Feisal next I'll talk to him, and the Arab attitude shall be sympathetic, for the duration of the war at least.' This was challenge enough, yet he also felt his own situation was becoming increasingly difficult. In the same letter he stated: 'I'm in an extraordinary position just now, vis à vis the Sherifs and the tribes, and sooner or later must go bust. I do my best to keep in the background, but cannot, and some day everybody will combine and down me. It is impossible for a foreigner to run another people of their own free will, indefinitely, and my innings has been a fairly long one.'

He was political and military adviser, but he was also, personally, the bearer of gold, sometimes undertaking long and exhausting journeys to lubricate the Revolt. Sherif Hussein's youngest son, Zeid, now active in the field but inexperienced and wilful, suddenly informed him that the money provided for the next phase of the campaign had already been squandered. Stunned by what he saw as 'the complete ruin of my plans and hopes, and the collapse of our effort to keep faith with Allenby', Lawrence hurried to Beersheba to hand in his resignation. There he learned of major new plans for the Palestine campaign which required precise and targeted help from Arab forces in view of which there was no possibility of Allenby and GHQ letting him go. 'There was no escape for me,' he wrote: 'I must take up again my mantle of fraud in the East.' Promotion and rewards failed to salve his unease. He wrote home on 8 March: 'They have given me a D.S.O. [i.e. the Distinguished Service Order for Tafileh]. It's a pity all this good stuff is not sent to someone who would use it! Also apparently I'm a colonel of sorts. Don't make any change in my address of course.' He was formally appointed 'Temporary Lieutenant Colonel' on the 12th. 'Colonel Lawrence' had arrived on the scene.

About this time, while visiting Jerusalem, he was introduced to a new arrival in the Middle East, the American journalist Lowell Thomas who was on the lookout for inspiring war stories in the East having singularly failed to find any in Europe. As Thomas put it in an interview many years later:

I encountered Lawrence first in one of Jerusalem's narrow streets. He was with some Arabs. He didn't look like an Arab to me. A little bit later I got in touch with the British Military Governor of Jerusalem – I called him the successor to Pontius Pilate – Sir Ronald Storrs, and I told Storrs about this group of Arabs, and one who was a blond, and wondered who he was. And Storrs opened the door to an adjoining room and there he was. And Storrs was the one who was responsible for labelling Lawrence, because he said to me: 'I want you to meet the uncrowned king of Arabia'.

Whether Storrs was indeed the first to fix the 'uncrowned king' tag to Lawrence is uncertain, but Thomas was sufficiently motivated by the encounter to follow him back to Arabia, together with his photographer-cum-cinematographer, Harry Chase. Thomas found it hard to extract much usable 'copy' from him since he insisted on giving all credit to Feisal and the other Arab leaders. He made better headway with some of Lawrence's fellow-officers, who were only too happy to divert the limelight in Lawrence's direction. All this would bear mixed fruit later on.

General Allenby's schemes seemed promising, but on 21 March, in France, the Germans launched the first of a series of powerful if increasingly desperate offensives, hoping to achieve a swift victory before the Americans were ready to engage their potentially limitless resources. Allenby's armies were instantly depleted to help Field Marshal Haig's, now fighting – in the latter's memorable phrase – with their 'backs to the wall'. Indian troops were promised to Allenby from Mesopotamia and elsewhere but these could not be integrated overnight. 'For the moment,' wrote Lawrence, 'we must both hold on.'

Realising that in view of the new stringency Allenby was about to dismount the Imperial Camel Corps in Sinai, Lawrence contrived to borrow two companies for a major foray in the desert. For once he was collaborating with British troops, on whom he made a powerful impression. Adopting a technique rare at the time he addressed each company in turn, giving them what Major Stirling called 'the straightest talk I ever heard... [They] retired for the night fully convinced that they were about to embark on the greatest jaunt in the history of war.'

Long delayed but meticuously planned, the final phase of the Palestine campaign, launched in September, took place at almost break-neck speed. While Allenby's armies mounted the massive main thrust along the coast, Feisal's forces advanced in parallel astride the Hejaz Railway. A major incident occurred when the retreating Turks massacred the inhabitants of Tafas, a village in their path, the headman of which, Sheikh Tallal, was with Lawrence's party. The occasion produced the last of *Seven Pillars*' high dramatic moments:

Tallal had seen what we had seen. He gave one moan like a hurt animal; then rode to the upper ground and sat there awhile on his mare, shivering and looking fixedly after the Turks... [T]hen he seemed suddenly to take hold of himself, for he dashed his stirrups into the mare's flanks and galloped headlong, bending low and swaying in the saddle, right at the main body of the enemy.

We sat there like stone while he rushed forward, the drumming of his hoofs unnaturally loud in our ears, for we had stopped shooting, and the Turks had stopped. Both armies waited for him; and he rocked on in the hushed evening till only a few lengths from the enemy. Then he sat up in his saddle and cried his war-cry, 'Tallal, Tallal', twice in a tremendous shout. Instantly their rifles and machine-guns crashed out, and he and his mare, riddled through and through with bullets, fell dead among the lance points.

Auda said, 'God give him mercy; we will take his price.' 'By my order', wrote Lawrence, 'we took no prisoners, for the only time in our war.'

There was indeed a savage killing, but a fellow officer junior to Lawrence,

Major Peake, arriving late on the scene, was personally ordered by him to round up as many prisoners as he could and guard them. By nightfall he had coralled 2,000. Peake's view was that Lawrence wished to take the guilt of any massacre on himself, in that having urged the Arabs to rebel it was only just that he should be blamed and not they.

Lawrence was especially eager that the Arabs should be at the forefront of the advance to Damascus and Allenby had agreed. The morning of 1 October found him heading at speed towards the city in the Rolls-Royce tender 'Blue Mist' from which he had been inseparable for some time, with Major Stirling at the wheel. Stopping by a stream for a wash and shave, they were briefly held under arrest by a patrol of Bengal lancers. Not possessing the necessary Urdu, they were released only through the chance meeting with a British officer to whom they were able to explain their identity, so they did not reach Damascus until 9 a.m. An unknown photographer caught what could be the moment of arrival, Lawrence himself leaning almost stiffly forward, alert, intense, if with a distinct air of fatigue belying any sense of triumph, his Arab dress dusty and dishevelled. Yet around him the city celebrated. This was not the progress of a British Colonel but of 'Urens', the Arabs' friend and champion. His name and those of Feisal, Nasir and of Shukri, the Arab whom Lawrence made temporary governor, ricocheted about the streets in the measured roar of many men's voices mingling with the local cries and the ullulation of women.

There are, it has to be said, other versions. The city was virtually surrounded by Allied troops, among which were the Australian cavalry who claim they got there first. Allenby delayed his own arrival to give Lawrence his chance, but he might also have come slowly because he had bad news to deliver, in that far from allowing Feisal his expected triumph in Damascus he was duty bound to prepare for a political takeover of Syria by the French. Either way Lawrence saw, as did his military master, that his role in the East was over. As he put it in his book: 'I made to Allenby the last (and also I think the first) request I ever made for myself – leave to go away'.

There was a strangely poignant final day during which the British war artist James McBey painted a portrait of him (see page 71), a remarkable interpretation, showing a man almost droop-eyed and sallow, half fallen in, which Lawrence would later describe as 'shockingly strange to me'. As McBey wielded his brushes various Arab leaders came in to him to kiss his hand and say farewell.

A key question remains. How important was the Arab contribution to the success of the Middle Eastern campaign? The distinguished Australian historian, Trevor Wilson, author of a recent authoritative history of Britain's contribution to the 1914–1918 conflict, *The Myriad Faces of War*, asserts that it had not been decisive, 'yet it had not been inconsiderable: in protecting Allenby's right flank, helping to mislead the enemy concerning the whereabouts of his initial thrust, and disrupting the Turks' communications.' Wilson also calls to witness General Glubb, famous as the last commander of the Arab Legion, in whose opinion 'the Arab Revolt was an extraordinary example of what could be achieved by guerrilla tactics. Tens of thousands of regular Turkish troops had been pinned down by an adversary barely capable of engaging a brigade of infantry in pitched battle. Such economy of force,' Wilson comments, 'was rare on either side in this war.'

Lawrence left Damascus on 4 October, travelling home by way of Egypt. 'The old war is closing, and my use is gone', he wrote from Cairo to the Base Commandant at Akaba, Major Scott, adding: 'We were an odd little set, and we have, I expect, changed History in the near East. I wonder how the Powers will let the Arabs get on.'

6

Political campaigner:
public celebrity

Lawrence returned to a country absorbed in the situation in Europe where at last
Germany and her allies were on the edge of defeat, but where, as across much of
the world, the influenza plague which had appeared earlier in the year and then
subsided was enjoying a massive resurgence. London in the autumn of 1918 was
a frightened city which lost 18,000 citizens to the so-called 'Spanish Flu' in a
matter of weeks; the capital's undertakers could hardly keep up with the demand
for coffins. Meanwhile the long casualty lists from the battle fronts filled their
usual newspaper columns, as they would continue to do for some weeks after
the Armistice of 11 November which effectively brought the war to its end.

Despite all this, Lawrence's voice pleading the Arabs' cause was allowed a
fair hearing. Following a brief visit to Oxford he was in London by 21 October
to appear before the War Cabinet's Eastern Committee, whose chairman was
Lord Curzon, now serving in Prime Minister Lloyd George's inner circle as Lord
President of the Council. The young officer's reputation had gone before him.
Curzon began by stating that 'he and every member of His Majesty's
Government had for some time watched with interest and admiration the great
work which Colonel Lawrence had been doing in Arabia, and felt proud that
[he] had done so much to promote the successful progress of the British and
the Arab arms.' When invited to give his own views, Lawrence did so without
equivocation. The minutes of the meeting stated: 'Colonel Lawrence's own idea
was the establishment of Abdullah as ruler of Baghdad and Lower Mesopotamia,
Zeid in a similar position in Upper Mesopotamia, with Feisal in Syria.'

He appeared before the Committee several times. A minute of a meeting on
27 November carried the significant comment: 'He is a man with a remarkable
career and of great ability, and he represented to us what we may call the extreme
Arab point of view, the kind of thing Faisal would have said if he had been at our

Previous page: The Emir Feisal at the
Paris Peace Conference; Lawrence,
above to his left, wearing an Arab
headdress. The third figure in the
photograph is the French artillery
officer Captain Pisani, who had also
participated in the Arab campaign.
Imperial War Museum, Q 55581

table that afternoon.' Praise, yet praise with a caution; the key word 'extreme'
carrying with it the distinct undertone that his suggestions might be listened to
with interest, but that they were unlikely to be carried out.

More publicly, though anonymously, he took his campaign to Fleet Street.
In late November *The Times* carried three major articles on three successive days by
'A Correspondent who was in close touch with the Arabs throughout their campaign against the Turks after the revolt of the Sherif of Mecca.' Their author made
no mention of his own role. In his covering letter to the Editor, Lawrence wrote:

*The Arabs came into the war without making a previous treaty with us, and have
consistently refused to listen to the temptations of other powers. They have never had a press
agent, or tried to make themselves out a case, but fought as hard as they could (I'll swear
to that) and suffered hardships in their three campaigns and losses that would break up
seasoned troops. They fought… without, I believe, any other very strong motive than a
desire to see the Arabs free.*

Lawrence's next transformation was arguably his most remarkable yet. It had
been agreed that Feisal should represent the views of the Arabs at the Paris Peace
Conference, due to begin in January 1919. Lawrence was assigned to accompany
him as translator, adviser and, effectively – though this role was largely self-
assigned – to handle his public relations. Frequently seen wearing an Arab headdress with his military uniform he amply justified Gertrude Bell's description
of him as the conference's 'most picturesque figure'. Yet this was not just self-
indulgent display. E.H.R.Altounyan would later comment that 'people of his kind
used themselves as they would use an animal or an instrument' simply in order
to get their way, sensing that 'it was a good thing for the cause that he should
be in the limelight'. Similarly, stories of what he had said to France's most senior

soldier, Marshal Foch, about the Crusades circulated among the delegates, all with the aim of creating publicity to gain his ends.

The misfortune was that, despite Lawrence and Feisal's efforts, the Arabs gained far less than they had hoped for. To the great powers the Arabs were small fry and should be grateful for anything offered them however unsatisfactory. His frustration was reflected in one of the first and finest paragraphs of *Seven Pillars of Wisdom*, in which he spoke not just for himself but for the whole war generation:

We lived many lives in those whirling campaigns, never sparing ourselves: yet when we achieved and the new world dawned, the old men came out again and took our victory to re-make in the likeness of the former world they knew. Youth could win, but had not learned to keep: and was pitiably weak against age. We stammered that we had worked for a new heaven and a new earth, and they thanked us kindly and made their peace.

In April 1919 Lawrence's father suddenly fell victim to influenza. Arnold wired his brother in Paris. Lawrence left immediately without telling Feisal, but arrived just too late. In what might seem a heartless gesture he went back to Paris before the funeral, if with a view to returning once he had cleared his visit with Feisal. This prompted a remarkable passage about his best British advocate in Feisal's personal diary:

The greatest thing I have seen in him, which is worthy of mention as one of his principal characteristics, is his patience, discretion, zeal and his putting the common good before his personal interest. When he came to take leave I asked him the reason for his departure. He said, 'I regret to say that my father has died and I want to go and see my mother.' I enquired when his father had died and he said, 'A week ago — I received a telegram saying that he was ill, and left straightway, but when I arrived I found that he had died two hours previously. I did not stay in England until the funeral because I realised that you were here alone and that there is much work to be done. I didn't want to be far from you, in case things happened in my absence. I didn't tell you this at the time in case it upset you, so I tell you now. I shall return on Friday'.

Feisal was much moved by what he saw as Lawrence's honesty, faithfulness, devotion to duty and control of personal feelings. 'These are the highest qualities of man,' he wrote, 'which are found in but few individuals.'

What makes this tribute the more telling is that even as it was being written the joint hopes of the two men, different in race yet united in commitment, were beginning to unravel. Feisal shortly returned to Syria, but not to claim a kingdom as Lawrence had hoped: rather to argue his case with a Middle Eastern Commission of Inquiry benign to the Arabs but which had little political clout. Eventually what he had long feared came to pass as the area fought over during the Revolt was divided between the British and French. Nothing so crude as annexation would be on the table; the newly invented convenience-phrase was 'mandate', a term specifically dated to 1919 and generally defined as 'the power conferred on a state to govern a region elsewhere'. The implication was that where a mandate was established a mature power would exercise a caring concern for peoples not quite ready for nationhood. In fact it was all but imperialism by stealth and a recipe for anger, frustration and endless trouble ahead.

Lawrence himself returned to the Middle East at this time. In spare hours in Paris he had started writing *Seven Pillars of Wisdom*. Though his book would never emerge as a straight documentary account he knew it needed a strong factual basis, the material for which was gathering dust in the offices of the Arab Bureau in Cairo. Hearing that the Royal Air Force – for which he had formed a serious

Feisal was much moved by what he saw as Lawrence's honesty, faithfulness, devotion to duty and control of personal feelings. 'These are the highest qualities of man,' he wrote, 'which are found in but few individuals.'

admiration during the last stages of the Palestine Campaign – was about to send six Handley Page bombers from France to Cairo he hitched a lift. Unfortunately his plane crashed at Rome killing its chief pilot with Lawrence lucky to escape with only a broken collarbone. He drafted the remarkable introductory chapter to *Seven Pillars* with his left arm in plaster during the remainder of his prolonged journey, which also included a brief interlude in Crete allowing a visit to the ruins of Knossos.

Meanwhile Oxford, where he had already been a member of two colleges, had offered him a home at a third. A Fellowship of All Souls College is an Oxford Oscar, providing a base, financial stability, and a scholarly ambience without the obligation to teach, or even to mingle with, the university's student population.

This was opportune in another way. With his father deceased, to resume regular residence at 2 Polstead Road would have put him in close contact with his mother, who was now mourning not only two of her sons but her unofficial husband as well. With Bob beyond reach in a religious world of his own and Arnold still in his teens, Lawrence would have been exposed to the full power of her domineering personality. As he would later admit in a letter to Charlotte Shaw (Mrs George Bernard Shaw, who was to become the principal confidante of his maturer years), Sarah Lawrence was forever 'hammering and sapping' to break into 'the circle of my integrity'. The woman who had long wanted to claim him for the Lord, who had frequently chastised him for his sins as a boy, would not be the easiest of companions as he faced his uncertain future.

But he was in the family home enough for Sarah (in a volume of reminiscences published after Lawrence's death) to bequeath a strangely disturbing image of her famous son at this period. Sometimes, she wrote, he would 'sit the entire morning between breakfast and lunch in the same position, without moving, and with the same expression on his face.' Exhaustion, both mental and physical? That ever-present sense of guilt? There might have been another factor about which she would necessarily have remained mute.

Preserved in the multitudinous papers of the Lawrence Collection in the Bodleian Library in Oxford is a letter which only came to light in recent years. It was written at some indeterminate time by Lawrence's father and reached to the heart of its subject without prevarication or preamble:

To my Sons,
(But not to be opened except Mother & I
are dead.) — OR when Mother desires to.

My dear Sons,
I know this letter will be a cause of great sorrow & sadness to you all, as it is to me to write it. The cruel fact is this, that yr mother & I were never married.
When I first met mother, I was already married. An unhappy marriage without love on either side tho' I had four young daughters. Yr Mother & I unfortunately fell in love with each other & when the exposé came, thought only of getting away & hiding ourselves with you Bob, then a baby. There was no divorce between my wife & myself. How often have I wished there had been! Then I drank & Mother had a hard time but happily I was able to cure myself of that. You can imagine or try to imagine how yr Mother & I have suffered all these years, not knowing what day we might be recognised by some one and our sad history published far and wide. You can think with what delight we saw each of you growing up to manhood, for men are valued for themselves & not for their family history, except of course under particular circumstances.

The letter went on to outline those 'circumstances' as here earlier described. There was some discussion of family financial arrangements, plus the information that Bob, their eldest, had been registered under the name of Chapman, though their father strongly recommended that he should retain the name Lawrence. The letter concluded, poignantly:

I can say nothing more, except that there never was a truer saying than 'the ways of transgressors are hard'. Take warning from the terrible anxieties & sad thoughts endured by both yr Mother and me for now over thirty years!

I know not what God will say to me (yr Mother is the least to be blamed) but I say most distinctly that there is no happiness in this life, except you abide in Him thro' Christ & oh I hope you all will.

Father

There is no indication as to when the letter was opened, but it is very possible that, their father having died, Sarah showed it to Ned at this period. Almost certainly it was never shown to Bob. As for Arnold, he would later admit that when he heard the truth about his parents he 'laughed heartily'; at which his brother retorted forcefully 'it was no joke for them'.

'The ways of transgressors are hard': if indeed he absorbed this moving confession at this juncture, when he at last had time to contemplate the highs and lows of his war, with its burden of political remorse and personal shame, it is not improbable that he might have experienced a sense of shock which for a while totally destabilised him. It is at least a plausible explanation of the uncharacteristic torpor described by his mother. Despite his claim to have known about the family's situation from his boyhood, this admission of the suffering that his parents had endured for so many years must have thrown a dark shadow across

Opposite: Lowell Thomas's highly
successful 'Illustrated Travelogue'
about the Middle Eastern campaign,
featuring General Allenby and 'Colonel
Thomas Lawrence', as reported in the
fashionable monthly magazine
The Sphere, in August 1919.
BL Newspaper Library, Colindale

the past in a way that he could hardly have imagined. His father had also
indicated in his letter that strictly he was Sir Robert Tighe Chapman, Baronet
(inviting his sons to confirm this, should they wish, in that bible of the
aristocracy, *Burke's Peerage*), though adding 'needless to say I have never taken the
Title'. To Lawrence, who had rubbed shoulders over years with so many of the
nation's élite while concealing his own pathetic illegitimacy, it must have seemed
galling to think how near he was to being one of them – in fact, a mere 'bend
sinister' away. Yet that gap was enough. In literature and history (and we are
discussing a widely read and deeply cultured man) the bastard was always the
villain, the malcontent in the wings: Edmund, not Edgar, in Shakespeare's
King Lear. That he should be doomed to this role – ever the lowly outsider,
the woodcutter, never the prince – must have bitten hard into his psyche.

He was also coming to terms with the realisation that there was no hope of
picking up where he had left off in 1914. Carchemish, apart from anything else
now under French control, was henceforward forbidden ground. He wrote sadly
to his Arabic tutor in the Lebanon, Fareedeh el Akle: 'I can't ever come to Syria
again. Because I failed.'

At this low point, Lowell Thomas strode back into his life, to affect it
for ever. The American's publicity visit to the Middle East was now bearing
remarkable fruit, in the shape of a dramatic travelogue entertainment which
included robust storytelling by Thomas – no mean performer – interwoven
with slides, music and dancing. First launched in New York, it opened at Covent
Garden in August 1919, delighting a London still in post-war shock with its
Oriental flair and flourish, playing to such huge audiences that it later moved to
and duly filled the Royal Albert Hall. Originally entitled *With Allenby in Palestine,
including the Capture of Jerusalem and the Liberation of Holy Arabia*, before long the

WITH GENERAL ALLENBY at Covent Garden Theatre.

A Remarkable Film Lecture Telling the Strange Story of Colonel Thomas Lawrence, the Leader of the Arab Army

Colonel Thomas Lawrence (on Left) with Mr. Lowell Thomas

Colonel Lawrence is here seen at the entrance to his tent with Mr. Lowell Thomas, the American journalist, who at Covent Garden is telling the story of the Arab campaign

Colonel Thomas Lawrence

When war broke out Thomas Lawrence was a young archæological student engaged in work on ancient Mesopotamian cities. His knowledge of Arabia was first made use of in the map department at Cairo, and finally we find him as leader of the whole Arab Army in its fight from Mecca to Damascus. He wore this Arab style of dress throughout the campaign, and gained the confidence of chiefs and followers alike. A price was set upon his head but Colonel Lawrence won through to Damascus at the head of a devoted army

   The Palestine Film Lecture at Covent Garden   *Drawn by D. Macpherson*

A large number of well-known personalities gathered on the opening night last week to hear Mr. Lowell Thomas's film lecture on the Palestine campaign. The lecturer showed pictures of Arab and other cavalry columns in motion which were quite unfamiliar to the man in the street

Mr. Lowell Thomas's wonderful pictures of the operations in Palestine, at Covent Garden, have revealed to many what a really big cavalry " show " means, and what it entails in the way of general organisation and detail, writes a military correspondent. Few laymen, at any rate in England, ever get the chance of seeing large bodies of cavalry massed for operations of war or of peace. In India, where there is elbow room and space, and where cavalry both on manœuvres and in the almost unending warfare on the N.-W. Frontier get more practice than any other cavalry in the world, we have, upon occasion, seen something of it. Ever since the times of what were called the " Kitchener tests," those of us who have served in India have had a taste of what the handling of large masses of Horse means. But even in India, when we perhaps had the equivalent of a cavalry division on manœuvres, it was a ceremonial parade compared to what this tremendous cavalry operation which Field-Marshal Lord Allenby conducted in Palestine connoted. These pictures, perhaps, brought home to the layman what it meant; they perhaps made him think of what it ,meant in terms of fodder, in terms of sore backs, and in terms of horse-shoes, quite apart from the little matter of the feeding and watering of both the horse and the man on his back. Good cavalry are supposed to be able to exist on the smell of an oil-rag; they are supposed to be able to fend for themselves if put to it.

Sometimes this thing is politely called " foraging," but people have also another name for it. Fending for yourself is possible when only a comparatively small body is involved; it is a different pair of shoes, however, when something very like a whole cavalry corps is on the warpath, as was the case in Palestine. Allenby started his service with the Inniskillings; he has been a cavalry soldier all his days, and the cavalry spirit has been breathed into him since the time when he first learnt how to " carry swords."

No one but a cavalry leader of such brilliance would have dared to conceive an operation of this magnitude over, such a country. Allenby, however, knew the quality of the cavalry he had under him—hunting yeomen from the " shires " and the " provinces," Anzacs who were bred in the saddle, Sikhs, Punjabs, Pathans, Gukkars from the Salt Range, natural horsemen, and, above all, horse-masters, every man Jack of them, and he took it on and knew that his Horse would not fail him. The most astounding fact to the cavalry soldier, who happens to know what it all meant, was the low percentage of casualties in horseflesh—on an all-round reckoning, less than 25 per cent. If the percentage had been 50 per cent. it would still have been a magnificent performance. As Mr. Lowell Thomas rightly adjudged, it is the most astonishing cavalry achievement in the whole history of war, ancient or modern.

My real wish is to ask if you will read, or try to read, a book which I have written. It's about the war, which will put you off, to start with, + there are technical unpleasantnesses about it. For instance it is very long: about 300 000 words I suspect, though I have not counted them. I have very little money + do not wish to publish it : however it had to be printed, so I got it done on a lino. press, in a newspaper office. That means it's beastly to look at, two columns on a quarto page, small newspaper type which hurts your eyes; + dozens of misprints, corrected roughly in ink: for only five copies exist, + I could not afford a proof. The punctuation is entirely the compositor's fancy : + he had an odd fancy, especially on Mondays.

That's the worst to be said on the material side. So far as concerns myself you must be told, before you commit yourself to saying "yes", that I'm not a writer, + successfully passed the age of 30 without having wanted to write anything. I was brought up as a professional historian, which means the worship of original documents. To my astonishment, after peace came I found I was myself the sole person who knew what had happened in Arabia during the war : + the only literate person in the Arab

focus had switched to 'Colonel Lawrence, the Leader of the Arab Army'; thus, effectively, 'Lawrence of Arabia' was born. Allenby went once and was given a standing ovation. Lawrence went several times, usually slipping in unseen. Typically his reaction to his growing fame was double-edged. He loved it and he loathed it. It was Thomas who devised a phrase about him which has stuck because of its simple aptness. He described Lawrence as 'backing into the limelight'.

Meanwhile he was wrestling with his book. Oxford inhibited his pen by too many distractions, even benign ones, such as his growing friendship with Robert Graves, an ex-warrior like himself who later became famous for his classic war memoir *Goodbye to All That* (and would also write Lawrence's first biography). Graves would recall serious talk with him but also undergraduate-like pranks; spotting from one of the higher levels of the nearby Bodleian Library a small crimson Hejaz flag fluttering from a pinnacle of All Souls College just across the road reminded him that his eccentric friend had been a notable roof-walker when at Jesus College before the war. In the event Lawrence was to find his best sanctum for writing not in Oxford but in London, in a top floor flat in 14 Barton Street, Westminster, where the nearest fluttering flags were those of a proud imperial capital. The flat was loaned to him by the architect Sir Herbert Baker, who had rented the premises from Westminster School. Here he could write at all hours in almost Trappist isolation, occasionally relaxing his hyperactive mind by nocturnal wanderings through the streets. 'I nearly went off my head in London this spring,' he told Graves, 'heaving at that beastly book of mine.'

Yet while trying to burn out his part in the desert war and thus dismiss it to the past, the Middle Eastern present suddenly reclaimed him for a major bout of political activity. In 1921 Winston Churchill, who was to conceive a lifelong admiration for Lawrence both as man of action and writer, was appointed

Colonial Secretary. He set out to remake the post-war settlement and called on Lawrence to assist him. He could not refuse. From early that year to the summer of 1922 Lawrence was a Colonial Office diplomat.

The product of Churchill's and Lawrence's efforts was not quite what the latter might have dreamed of during his desert rides. The Grand Sherif held out for more than he was offered and was forced to abdicate; but after a long exile in Cyprus, he achieved his wish to end his days on Islamic soil, dying in Amman in 1931 and being buried in Jerusalem in the Dome of the Rock. Nevertheless, out of the 1922 settlement Mesopotamia emerged as Iraq, an autonomous kingdom under Feisal, while Abdullah became effectively ruler of Transjordan (today the Kingdom of Jordan). Writing to Graves in 1927, Lawrence claimed that the settlement these dispositions represented were 'the big achievement of my life: of which the war was a preparation'. In the only footnote in *Seven Pillars* (chapter 48), he wrote of being 'quit of our war-time Eastern adventure with clean hands', yet one can't help surmising that even while using such a phrase he might have heard over his shoulder the guilty musings of a Lady Macbeth, whose hand, as Shakespeare has it in his play, all the perfumes of Arabia could not sweeten. After all, Syria was effectively French, while Palestine was to most intents and purposes British. The Arab–Israeli conflict was far off, although the roots of it were already taking hold.

His diplomatic mission completed, Lawrence abruptly resigned and astonished supporters and doubters alike by changing his name and joining the

The 1921 Cairo Peace Conference: Winston Churchill, Colonial Secretary, seated centre, with his advisers, sometimes jokingly known as the 'forty thieves'. Lawrence, for once photographed in suit and tie, stands behind Churchill and to his left. Also included, second row second left, is the famous Middle Eastern traveller and writer Gertrude Bell.
Hulton Getty

Royal Air Force, not as an officer but in the ranks. Suddenly the popular hero and celebrity had dropped into an oubliette and was lost from view. It was almost as if Dumas's morality tale was reversed and the Count of Monte Cristo had locked himself away in the Château d'If. The years of hide-and-seek had begun.

7

It was arguably the strangest disappearing act in modern British history. It might have been more easily understood if he had converted to Catholicism and entered a monastery.

Changes of identity

It was arguably the strangest disappearing act in modern British history. It might have been more easily understood if he had converted to Catholicism and entered a monastery. But his faith had diminished over the years and he was no longer at ease with orthodox religion, so he sought a contemporary lay version of withdrawal. There being no possibility of a Brother Lawrence, suddenly there was an ordinary airman answering to the unlikely name of John Hume Ross. The name – a total invention – was, of course, immaterial; the whole point of his alias was anonymity. He might as easily have enlisted as Aircraftman Nemo.

There was at least a reasonable pretext for joining the Air Force since he had come to admire it for its contribution to the Middle Eastern campaign. Yet once he donned R.A.F. uniform, there were few signs of any great interest in the element to which the zealots of this newborn discipline were beginning to lay claim. The new recruit grimly square-bashing at the rigorous basic-training establishment that was R.A.F. Uxbridge had no ambition to play a role in the development of air power; indeed, he was doing his best to fade into the crowd. He did have another ambition, however; to find in the Air Force the means of satisfying a chronic, irresistible desire to create another book.

Lawrence would in time become the friend of many distinguished writers – among them Bernard Shaw, John Buchan, Siegfried Sassoon and Thomas Hardy – but one with whom he formed an especially valued relationship was the novelist, E.M. Forster. Forster would find *Seven Pillars* a useful stimulus when struggling to complete his most successful and famous work *A Passage to India*. But Forster had a gift that Lawrence felt had been denied him; he was a creative writer, and Lawrence was not. He once wrote to him: 'You can rule a line, as hard as this pen-stroke, between the people who are artists and the rest of the world'; and he knew where he stood – with the rest of the world. This recognition that he was

Previous page: Lawrence in the second
of his Royal Air Force identities,
Aircraftman T.E. Shaw, photographed
in Miranshah, India, December 1928.
By this time Shaw was his correct name,
legally acquired by deed-poll.
Bodleian Library

incapable of creating fiction meant that the only alternative was to put himself
into a non-fiction situation worth chronicling. The accident of war had given
him the Arab Revolt; now he himself chose the R.A.F., having pleaded his case
for joining with the Chief of Air Staff himself, the legendary Sir Hugh, later
Lord, Trenchard. 'I can't do this without your help. I'm 33 and not skilled in the
senses you want... You'll wonder what I'm at. The matter is that since I was 16
I've been writing: never satisfying myself technically but steadily getting better.
My last book on Arabia is nearly good. I see the sort of subject I need in the
beginning of your Force... and the best place to see a thing from is the ground.
It wouldn't "write" from the officer level.'

It was a correct prediction. Scribbling detailed notes almost daily, recording
every sensation from listening to the night noises in the barrack-room to coping
with the Monday morning shit-cart, he carved out of his R.A.F. experiences a
book picturing low-life from within that has been bracketed with works by such
writers as Dostoevsky, Orwell or Solzhenitsyn. If Trenchard was led to expect an
enthusiast's portrait of the service that was effectively his child (he was, after all,
known as the 'Father' of the R.A.F.), *The Mint* was anything but that. With every
four-letter word known to man freely included, it was unpublishable as written
and Lawrence knew it; in fact he instructed in his will that it should not be
published before 1950. In 1936 his brother A.W. Lawrence had fifty copies
printed, not for publication, but to secure United States copyright. It appeared in
its first public edition, carefully expurgated, in 1955, not being published in full
until 1973.

But the urge to write was one motive among many for his sudden plunge
out of the limelight. In a letter to Robert Graves in November 1922, he listed
various others. It was 'a necessary step, forced on me by an inclination towards

ground-level: by a despairing hope that I'd find myself on common ground with men: by a little wish to become more human than I had become in Barton Street: by an itch to make myself ordinary in a mob of likes; also I'm broke…' Cutting through the maze of reasons he concluded, brusquely: 'I wanted to join up, that's all: and I am still glad, sometimes, that I did. It's going to be a brain-sleep, and I'll come out of it less odd than I went in: or at least less odd in other men's eyes.'

He wrote this from his second station, Farnborough, the home of the R.A.F. School of Photography. On arriving there he had soon made a life-long friend of his hut orderly, an ex-Royal Navy rough diamond known as 'Jock' Chambers, who began by calling him 'Shortarse' and making him scrub his bed-space twice before pronouncing himself satisfied, but within weeks was proving his valiant champion when his true identity was suddenly outed by the Press. Headlines such as 'Uncrowned King as Private Soldier', or 'Prince of Mecca on Rifle Parade' had Fleet Street's reporters down in droves. Chambers was with 'A/C Ross' when they were approached by two of them, one of whom asked Lawrence, who was standing on guard, 'You don't happen to be him, do you?', to which Lawrence disarmingly replied, 'Now, do I look like a soldier?' 'That was all there was to it,' Chambers stated, recalling the incident. 'This bloke just walked away.'

Nevertheless, the furore was such that by the end of January 1923 Lawrence was a civilian again. He told his literary adviser and friend Edward Garnett: 'The R.A.F. have sacked me for the crime of possessing too wide a publicity for a ranker.' But he would not be deterred, and within two months he had enlisted as a Private in the Tank Corps, under a new alias, that of Thomas Edward Shaw, and was posted to the Tank Corps' training camp at Bovington, near Wareham, in Dorset. (This variation of his identity at least restored his original initials, T.E., by

God, this is awful. For two hours up and down the filthy street, lips and hands and knees tremulously out of control, my heart pounding with fear of that little door, through which I must go to join up. Try sitting a moment in the churchyard. That's caused it. The nearest lavatory, now. Oh, yes, under the church, of course. What was that story about the cornice?

A penny : and that leaves me fifteen. Buck up, old seat-wiper ; I can't tip you, and I'm urgent. Won by a short head. My right shoe is burst along the welt, and my trousers are growing fringes. One reason I always swore I wasn't a man of action was this routine running of the bowels before a crisis. However, now we end it. I'm going straight in.

All smooth so far. They are gentle spoken, almost sorry, to us. Won't you walk into my parlour ? "Wait here for your medical exam." Righto. That sodden pyramid of clothes upon the floor shows there's a man in front who's dirtier than me. My go next ? Everything off ? Ross ? That's me. "D'you smoke ?"... "Not much, Sir". "Well, cut it out ; see ?" (About six months back, it was, my last cigarette. However, no use to give myself away " Your Nerves are very bad " The Scotch-voiced doctor's hard fingers go hammer, hammer, hammer over the loud box of my ribs. I must be pretty hollow. "Turn over : get up : lift your right leg : hold it there : cough : all right: on your toes : arms straight in front of you : open your fingers wide : hold them so : turn round : hullo, what's these marks ? Punishment ? " No, Sir, persuasion, Sir, I think." Face, neck, chest getting hot.

"Hum, that would account for the nerves." His voice sounds softer , now. "Don't put them down, Mac. Say— two parallel scars on ribs— what were they, Boy ?""Superficial wounds, Sir." "Answer my question" "A barbed-wire tear out hunting " "Hum....and how long have you been short of food ?" O Lord, I never thought he'd spot that. Since April I've taken what meals I dared off my friends: all my shame would let me take. I'd walk down the Duke of York's steps at lunch time, so as to turn back with someone to his club for the food whose necessity nearly choked me. Still he needn't know all that.

"Gone a bit short the last three months, Sir." "More like six" in a growl. The worst of telling lies naked is that the red shows all down one's body. A long pause. Oh, I wish I hadn't taken this job on... At last "All right, get back into your clothes. You aren't as good as we want, but after a few weeks at the Depot you'll pull up all right." "Thank you very much, Sir." "Best of luck, boy," from Mac. Grunt from the kinder-spoken one. Here's the vegetable market again, still here. I'm still shaking all over. I've done it anyhow. There's a Fuller's down there. I've a mind to blow my shilling on a coffee. It's six years before I've got to think of a meal.

1 : RECRUITING OFFICE

GOD, this is awful. Hesitating for two hours up and down a filthy street, lips and hands and knees tremulously out of control, my heart pounding in fear of that little door through which I must go to join up. Try sitting a moment in the churchyard? That's caused it. The nearest lavatory, now. Oh yes, of course, under the church. What was Baker's story about the cornice?

A penny; which leaves me fifteen. Buck up, old seat-wiper: I can't tip you and I'm urgent. Won by a short head. My right shoe is burst along the welt and my trousers are growing fringes. One reason that taught me I wasn't a man of action was this routine melting of the bowels before a crisis. However, now we end it. I'm going straight up and in.

★

All smooth so far. They are gentle-spoken to us, almost sorry. Won't you walk into my parlour? Wait upstairs for medical exam? 'Righto!' This sodden pyramid of clothes upon the floor is sign of a dirtier man than me in front. My go next? Everything off? (Naked we come into the R.A.F.). Ross? 'Yes, that's me.'

Officers, two of them. . . .

'D'you smoke?'

Not much, Sir.

'Well, cut it out. See?'

Six months back, it was, my last cigarette. However, no use giving myself away.

'Nerves like a rabbit.' The scotch-voiced doctor's hard fingers go hammer, hammer, hammer over the loud box of my ribs. I must be pretty hollow.

13

which many of his friends came to know him from this time forward. His new surname was not in any way associated with Bernard Shaw the playwright; it appears that the choice was purely coincidental.)

Dorset suited him, eventually providing him with a permanent home. The camp was at the heart of Thomas Hardy's Egdon Heath, a wilderness of gorse and bracken and whale-back hills; cliffs and the sea lay just beyond. Tanks scoured the countryside, leaving great swathes of sand and gouged-out wadis almost like fragments of desert. Narrow roads criss-crossed the heathland, offering numerous opportunities for a new interest that virtually became a craze, Brough Superior Motor-Cycles, the acme of motorised two-wheeled transport at that time.

So much was positive, but he disliked the army from the start and made no secret of it. 'Wish I could see you,' he wrote to Chambers, 'am home-sick for the R.A.F. The army is more beastly than anything else which the wit of man has made.' He had found his Air Force comrades 'the cleanest little mob of fellows', as he called them in a letter to his Oxford friend Lionel Curtis, in spite of their being 'foul-mouthed'. His new barrack-mates were equally lewd, but in a crucially different manner. 'Behind their mouths is a pervading animality of spirit, whose unmixed bestiality frightens me and hurts me.'

In one of his most searing letters, again to Curtis, in which his ambivalent attitude to his own birth lurks like a dark undertow, he wrote:

I lie in bed night after night with this cat-calling carnality seething up and down the hut, fed by streams of fresh matter from twenty lecherous mouths,... and my mind aches with the rawness of it... We are all guilty alike, you know. You wouldn't exist, I wouldn't exist, without this carnality. Everything with flesh in its mixture is the achievement of a moment when the lusty thought of Hut 12 has passed to action and conceived; and isn't it true that

His new barrack-mates were equally lewd, but in a crucially different manner. 'Behind their mouths is a pervading animality of spirit, whose unmixed bestiality frightens me and hurts me.'

the fault of birth rests somewhat on the child? I believe it's we who led our parents on to bear us, and it's our unborn children who make our flesh itch.

He would later find good friends among these men, but to begin with he saw them as a ragbag of drop-outs and failures and himself as no better than they. Adding to his distress was the knowledge that if he wished he could leave the Army at any moment. 'It's terrible to hold myself voluntarily here:' he told Curtis, 'and yet I want to stay here till it no longer hurts me: till the burnt child no longer feels the fire.'

Sometime during his period in the Tank Corps Lawrence must have initiated the punishment beatings of which the public became aware only many years after his death. What the precise reason for them was must remain unknowable, but it is generally assumed they were associated with Deraa, both the agony and the shaming sexual pleasure of that traumatic episode. To A. W. Lawrence they were arguably a variant of medieval flagellation, the condign punishment for guilt and sin; others have seen in them evidence of a perverted homosexuality – though it should be said that the homosexual assumption could infuriate servicemen with whom he had shared barrack rooms. Another partial explanation, perhaps, is that feats of extreme endurance were always necessary to him, that behind the middle-aged man under the birch we can discern the teenage bicyclist thrusting south towards the Mediterranean, the undergraduate seeing how long he could go without food, the desert raider showing he could equal if not beat the Bedouin in their own terrain. In a telling sentence in the Oxford edition of his book, he wrote of the desert campaign: 'Pain became an allurement, like danger'. Life for him had to be on the edge, just as on his motorcycle he diced consciously with the dangers of speed. Whatever the cause, Bovington provided a suitable accomplice in the person of a fellow Tank Corps soldier named John

Lawrence's cottage at Clouds Hill, in its private dell. He once wrote of it to Lady Astor: '[It] is as ugly as my sins, bleak, angular, small, unstable: very like its creator. Yet I love it.' The cottage is now the property of the National Trust.
Author photograph

Bruce, prepared to accommodate him in these grim rituals, which were to continue on and off over the following years.

His first years at Bovington seem almost to have threatened Lawrence's mental balance. In the letter to Curtis above quoted he admitted: 'Sometimes I wonder how far mad I am, and if a mad-house would not be my next (and merciful) stage.'

Fortunately, instead of a mad house he found a half derelict one a mile or so to the north of the camp at Clouds Hill (strictly the name applies not to the building but to the area). It stood on a piece of land recently leased to a Tank Corps Army sergeant, Arthur Knowles, who was building his own bungalow across the road while also fulfilling an obligation to restore the old house at the same time. Lawrence opened negotiations and soon agreed terms. By November he was writing to Jock Chambers: 'I'm not wholly resourceless in Bovington: found a ruined cottage near camp and took it for 2/6 a week. Have roofed it and am flooring it. At present one chair and a table there... No floor-scrubbing. Scruffy place. About a dozen good books already.' The connection with the Knowles family would continue, Arthur's son Pat later becoming a supportive combination of neighbour, friend and − almost − unofficial batman whenever Lawrence was at Clouds Hill.

At first it was a bolthole rather than a place to live − he slept in camp − but he could spend his evenings there and it would be ideal for the literary activities for which he now needed to find time. With *The Mint* on hold after leaving the R.A.F. he had kept his mind active that summer by translating a novel, *The Forest Giant*, from the French. He had also decided to bring his last labours on *Seven Pillars* to a head, not by preparing a version for general publication, but by creating a 'subscribers' only' edition, to be produced to the highest possible standards of printing, illustration and design – applying his youthful dreams of fine book production to his own work. Playing the dual role of war-hero and self-appointed outcast which he frequently adopted in his service years, the lowly Army Private enlisted the aid of an expatriate American printer, Manning Pike, and a cadre of top British artists, including Augustus John, Eric Kennington, William Roberts, Paul Nash and Henry Lamb.

The cottage provided a suitable retreat for working in but it also offered the prospect of solitariness and ease. 'I covet the idea' he wrote to a wartime colleague, 'of being sometimes by myself near a fire.' Essentially it was a new version of his garden sanctum in Polstead Road; the hermit's private cell, the hideaway from the pressures of the world for which he always craved. In a letter to Charlotte Shaw dated March 1924, he admitted as much: he could now 'hide a quiet while in a cloud-defended cottage'.

Defended by clouds but also by a spontaneous exuberance of nature. The cottage stood in its own secluded dell, an arena of grass and gravel dominated by high hedgerows, bushes and trees. There was gorse in abundance, broom, laurel, bush heather, honeysuckle; daffodils, primroses and periwinkles in season, while among and beyond were oaks, silver birch, fir trees of numerous varieties heaped up to the summit of the hill. The most dominant presence was that of the rhododendrons. Initially suspicious, by the following summer he had yielded to them. He wrote to Charlotte Shaw: 'The cottage is nearly closed in with mountains of rhododendron bloom, of the screaming blue-pink which I used to dislike: now that they are my plants I love them.'

It was a sanctuary for him, but it was also a place to share. He brought congenial fellow soldiers from the camp there, and various literary friends came to join the select company. Prominent among the latter was E.M. Forster, who, he

AS I walked northward towards the fighting, Abdulla met me, on his way to Zeid with news. He had finished his ammunition, lost five men from shell-fire, and had one automatic gun destroyed. Two guns, he thought the Turks had. His idea was to get up Zeid with all his men and fight: so nothing remained for me to add to his message; and there was no subtlety in leaving alone my happy masters to cross and dot their own right decision.

He gave me leisure in which to study the coming battlefield. The tiny plain was about two miles across, bounded by low green ridges, and roughly triangular, with my reserve ridge as base. Through it ran the road to Kerak, dipping into the Hesa valley. The Turks were fighting their way up this road. Abdulla's charge had taken the western or left-hand ridge, which was now our firing-line.

Shells were falling in the plain as I walked across it, with harsh stalks of wormwood stabbing into my wounded feet. The enemy fuzing was too long, so that the shells grazed the ridge and burst away behind. One fell near me, and I learned its calibre from the hot cap. As I went they began to shorten range, and by the time I got to the ridge it was being freely sprinkled with shrapnel. Obviously the Turks had got observation somehow, and looking round I saw them climbing along the eastern side beyond the gap of the Kerak road. They would soon outflank us at our end of the western ridge.

460

Opposite: Lawrence in despair; part of
his moving letter to Mrs Charlotte Shaw
after his traumatic meeting with King
Feisal in 1925.
The British Library, Add. MS 45903, f.68

later recorded, 'liked the place at once. I felt easy – and to feel easy was, in T.E.'s eyes, a great recommendation. We weren't to worry about the world and the standards the world imposes.' 'What was Clouds Hill?' Lawrence wrote to Charlotte Shaw after an evening of records and conversation in 1924: 'A sort of mixed grill, I fancy: but very good. Everybody is beginning to fall in love with it. The air of it is peaceful: and the fire burns so well.'

Yet, for all its virtues, Clouds Hill did not reconcile him to life in the Tank Corps. He longed to return to his preferred service. He wrote to Trenchard: 'Have I no chance of re-enlistment in the R.A.F., or transfer? It remains my only hope and ambition, dreamed of every week, nearly every day.' He began to hint at suicide if he failed to get his way, creating a panic in high places which even drew in the Prime Minister, Stanley Baldwin. On 16 July 1925, Trenchard signed the order approving his transfer. 'This pleases me,' he wrote next day to a friend, 'it's like going home.' By August, mounted on his latest Brough Superior motorcycle, he was thundering up the Great North Road in the direction of the R.A.F. Cadet College at Cranwell, Lincolnshire.

'A very comfortable, peaceful camp' was the verdict of 338171 Aircraftman Shaw, which rank and number he would retain for the rest of his service. Yet, before long, he was in despair again. An invitation by a former wartime colleague, Lord Winterton, to a lunch at his country home in Surrey with Feisal, now King of Iraq, tore open barely healed psychological wounds. Small-talk about old times was impossible to him. 'I've changed', he wrote, in an anguished letter to Charlotte Shaw, 'and the Lawrence who used to go about and be friendly and familiar with that sort of people is dead. He's worse than dead. He is a stranger I once knew.' The occasion awakened in him an alarming sense that 'I've crashed my life and self and gone hopelessly wrong... O dear, O dear, what a coil.'

Cranwell

28. IX. 25

Do you know what it is when you see, suddenly, that your life is all a ruin? Tonight it is cold, & the hut is dark & empty, with all the fellows out somewhere. Every day I haunt their company, because the noise stops me thinking. Thinking drives me mad, because of the invisible ties about me which limit my moving, my wishing, my imagining. All these bonds I have tied myself, deliberately, wishing to tie myself down beyond the hope or power of movement. And this deliberation, this intention, rests. It is stronger than anything else in me, than everything else put together. So long as there is breath in my body my strength will be exerted to keep my soul in prison, since nowhere else can it exist in safety. The terror of being run away with, in the liberty of power, lies at the back of these many renunciations of my later life. I am afraid, of myself. Is this madness?

The trouble tonight is the reaction against yesterday, when I went mad :— rode down to London, spent a night in a solitary bed, in a furnished bed-room, with an old woman to look after the house about me : and called in the morning on Feisal, whom I found lively, happy to see me, friendly, curious. He was due for lunch at Winterton's (Winterton, with me during the war, is now U.S. of S. for India). We drove there together, and had lunch in Winterton's lovely house, a place of which I'm

At least Cranwell gave him the space in which to finish his labours on *Seven Pillars*. The distribution of his long-awaited masterwork to its subscribers could now begin. But another cloud loomed. In order to clear debts accrued in making that edition, he had agreed to the publication of a 'cadet' version of the book, stripped of its agony and ecstasy, to appear under the imprint of Jonathan Cape with the eye-catching title of *Revolt in the Desert*. This would clearly be a bestseller and unleash the press-hounds yet again. Lawrence asked the R.A.F. to forestall the inevitable publicity by allowing him to disappear, and by December he was on the S.S. *Derbyshire* heading for India, relieved in one sense but also 'lamenting Cranwell and England, and all good things'.

January 1927 saw his arrival at the Aircraft Depot at Drigh Road, Karachi (at that time part of India), a base selected by the R.A.F. authorities as a suitably obscure posting for the service's most awkward and controversial member. His work, as little more than a clerk, allowed him to keep the lowest of profiles. He wrote to Trenchard's Secretary T.B. Marson: 'I am attempting a hard thing: to make the camp suffice for my needs. I haven't been outside its bounds since I arrived: a sort of voluntary C.B.' 'C.B.' meant 'Confined to Barracks' – a well-known punishment for military misbehaviour.

The reasons for this self-imposed confinement brought about a major confrontation with the question of his identity. Clearly his popular reduction could not be published under any other authorship than that of the well-known war hero. He sought a suitable compromise by locking the now hated name in inverted commas as though it were a pseudonym. So *Revolt in the Desert* is by 'T.E Lawrence' (just as Liddell Hart's biography, published some years later, was given the title *'T.E. Lawrence' in Arabia and After*). More, that summer in Karachi he took the step of disowning T.E. Lawrence for good. On 16 June he wrote to his solicitor, the Honourable Edward Eliot: 'I want to change my name formally. Will you try and do it as quietly and inexpensively as it can be done? I'd better be Thomas Edward Shaw in future'

In the previous month, he had written a notable letter to Dr A.E. Cowley, 'Bodley's Librarian' (i.e. head of Oxford's Bodleian Library) about the copy of the subscribers' edition of *Seven Pillars of Wisdom* which the Library would shortly receive. As, intentionally, it carried no author's name, he had anticipated problems as to how it might be accessioned: 'You'll have to index it under Shaw, that being my initials in it. God help the catalogue with me, some day, for not even Lawrence is the correct and authentic name which I will eventually have to resume. I've published as Lawrence, as Shaw, as Ross: and will, probably, eventually publish as C. What a life!'

'C', of course, meant 'Chapman': now in his letter to Eliot he made his expectations, or perhaps his hopes, even clearer, stating that Shaw might be an 'intermediate stage' only, '*for eventually, I suppose, Chapman it will have to be.* [author's italics]. He continued: 'There is a lot of land in that name knocking about: and I don't want to chuck it away, as Walter Raleigh, for whom I have a certain regard, gave it to my father's first Irish ancestor. I have a feeling it should be kept in the line.'

The conclusion is unavoidable, surely, that Lawrence hoped somehow to be restored to that line, to be grafted back into the family tree: in effect, to be legitimised. His elder brother had been named Chapman, why should he not claim the name too? Why could he not in time throw off his various aliases, and secure himself once and for all to respectable, long-established roots? Coincidentally while in India he began a translation of Homer's *Odyssey* at the request of a distinguished American book designer and typographer, Bruce

Rogers. His comment made subsequently to David Garnett that his translation should really be called 'Chapman's Homer' was perhaps not the quip it was generally taken to be.

Lawrence rarely sentimentalised about his years in Arabia, but a letter written from Karachi in October 1927 to his former comrade-in-arms, Major Peake, now commanding the Arab Legion in Transjordan under the sobriquet of 'Peake Pasha', drew from him a comment that revealed an almost palpable nostalgia: 'I wonder if you still ride up and down that delectable land. I am often hungry for another sight of its hills. Rumm, too. If only…' But this is a significant letter in more ways than one. To anyone brought up with an awareness of John Bunyan's *Pilgrim's Progress*, as Lawrence undoubtedly was – he often carried a copy with him, to read or to lend – the word 'delectable' carries an immediate, potent resonance. The 'Delectable Mountains' were a benign landmark on the long and dangerous journey of Bunyan's hero Christian to the Celestial City, offering respite after such hazards as the Slough of Despond, the Valley of Humiliation and Doubting Castle. It would be strange indeed if Lawrence did not recognise certain remarkably close parallels in his own pilgrimage.

In May 1928 he left Karachi for Peshawar and was then posted to the remote station of Miranshah, on the North West Frontier. 'I like this place,' he wrote to E.M. Forster, 'it feels as though I'd dropped over the world's rim out of sight.' He was as much absorbed in his *Odyssey* as in his office work and was almost content. Then, suddenly, nearby Afghanistan found itself in crisis. A revolt against the King put that frequently troubled country into the world's headlines. This, together with the fact that the fomenter of the Arab Revolt was in the region under an assumed name was too much for a press always ready for a scoop about the 'arch-spy of the world'. Clearly Lawrence was up to his old tricks again. The *Empire News* of Manchester spun the story, other newspapers such as the *Daily Herald* ran with it, while – symbolic of a rising culture of protest that saw evil in any Western tampering with emergent nations – in London anti-imperialists burned him in effigy on Tower Hill. The R.A.F. and the Government of India decided they had no alternative but to fetch their one-man awkward squad home. On his arrival in February 1929 a flotilla of small boats packed with pressmen attempted to ambush his liner, the SS *Rajputana*, when it steamed into Plymouth Sound, so that he had to be spirited off the ship in a fast pinnace and rushed by car up to London.

Early February 1929 found him holed up in Barton Street and back to his old habits of night-walking the Empire's and the nation's capital. He wrote to T.B. Marson: 'For the moment I wander about London with my eyes on the pavement, like a man who's dropped sixpence, and can't remember in which street it was.' He added: 'On March 8 I move to Cattewater (Plymouth) which is to be my next camp. I hope it will prove a homely place.'

8

'I sit in camp, busy (more or less) on
some ghastly scrounge, and read that
I'm making rebellion in Persia. It's
only human to smile broadly: and
there'd be nothing but fun in it if my
chiefs were not so sensitive.'

Journey's end

The R.A.F. Flying Boat station at Cattewater on Plymouth Sound was indeed
to prove a homely, even a happy, posting. Its Commanding Officer was Wing-
Commander Sydney Smith, who had masterminded Lawrence's secret dash from
Plymouth to London, and he, his wife Clare and their daughter Maureen (known
as 'Squeak') became close friends. Linked both by their recent escapade and an
earlier acquaintance in the East during Lawrence's Colonial Office period, he
and Smith were also united in their dislike of the base's infelicitous name and
managed to persuade the Air Ministry to replace it with the name of a nearby
pier and call it Mount Batten. He became increasingly confident that the press
would invent no more yarns, and in July he felt relaxed enough to write to
a friend: 'All's looking well for a peaceful old age'.

Then one morning in December 1929 he awoke to find himself the subject
of another newspaper absurdity. He turned for help to Charles Pennycook
('Robbie') Robertson, head of the Press and Publicity Branch of the Air Ministry.
He wrote in some heat: 'I sit in camp, busy (more or less) on some ghastly
scrounge, and read that I'm making rebellion in Persia. It's only human to smile
broadly: and there'd be nothing but fun in it if my chiefs were not so sensitive.'
There was genuine worry in his response, his fear being that the next press
furore might prove a scandal too far, that the ghost of his expulsion from R.A.F.
Farnborough might reappear to haunt him. His letter also contained a brusque
hands-off to an American journalist who had asked Robertson to arrange an
interview about the desert war, but there was a tiny jewel of revelation wrapped
in the rebuttal: 'As for the Arabs, do tell your sportsman that he is out of date. It
was about ten or twelve years ago and I've forgotten all about it. You handle Arabs,
I think, as you handle Englishmen, or Laplanders or Czechoslovaks: cautiously,
at first, and kindly always.'

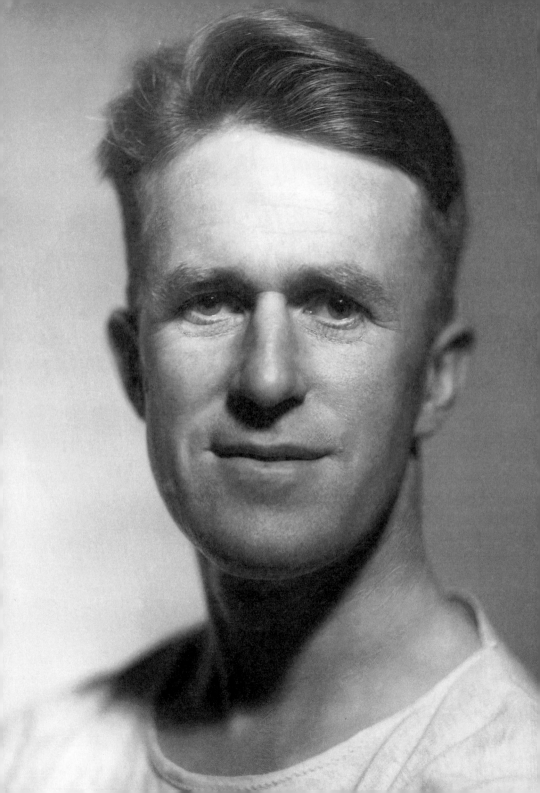

Previous page: Lawrence, October 1931, as portrayed by the photographer Howard Coster, who met Lawrence by chance and asked to photograph him; Lawrence agreed, he told Mrs Shaw, 'for the joke of it'. Coster took several fine close-ups, including this one, rarely published, showing Lawrence in a remarkably relaxed and cheerful mood.
National Portrait Gallery

Yet the publicity furore soon subsided. Indeed, the years that followed his posting to Mount Batten saw, for much of the time, an almost contented T.E. Lawrence, enjoying the relative obscurity of his now legal alias T.E. Shaw. Lurking demons would never be entirely dismissed, but the worrying intellectual evolved into a less troubled, less ambitious person capable of working with a satisfying combination of hand and brain. Wing-Commander Smith involved him as a member of an R.A.F. support team for the Schneider Cup seaplane contest of 1929, one by-product of which was the acquisition of a tiny American speedboat which Lawrence managed to repair. Its grateful owner later gave it to him and Smith as a souvenir. Named *The Biscuit*, it provided much enjoyment as its high-throated engine became a familiar sound in the waters around Mount Batten and the mouth of the River Tamar.

This provoked an interest in Lawrence in high-speed boats, but a more pivotal event occurred in February 1931 when he saw an Iris flying-boat crash 600 yards offshore while coming into Plymouth Sound. The boat launched by the Mount Batten staff in response proved cumbersome and slow, and by the time Lawrence and the rest of the rescue team reached the scene six lives had been lost. Distressed by this failure Wing-Commander Smith urged the Air Ministry to create faster tenders and Lawrence soon found himself drafted into a team working on new designs at the British Power Boat Company on Southampton Water. He admitted to an artist friend in April 1932: 'Books have not lain much in my way, lately; when dark comes I am tired, more inclined to read the *Happy Magazine* than Plato. So I compromise by reading neither, and am the better mechanic therefor.'

'Friendship is all the house I have' wrote the poet W.B. Yeats in one of his best loved poems, and while Lawrence had Clouds Hill he also had an increasing

'house' of close and caring friends and this was the high period of them. He was an equally welcome visitor to Bernard and Charlotte Shaw at Ayot St Lawrence, to John Buchan at Elsfield near Oxford, or to Lady Astor, at Plymouth where she was an M.P., or at Cliveden where she presided over the most exclusive set in England. Lady Astor even developed a passion for riding pillion on his motorcycle. Once on a wild wet morning he roared across Dartmoor to North

Devon to meet the novelist Henry Williamson, famous for his recently-published classic *Tarka the Otter*, astonishing his host with the force of his personality within seconds of struggling out of the minesweeper's suit he had been travelling in. On another occasion when near Manchester, testing yet another new Brough, he 'swirled off to spend the day' with a former member of the Royal Flying Corps and comrade of wartime days, B.E. Leeson, on the off-chance he might be lunching at home. 'Only, of course, you were not', as he was courteously informed by Leeson's maid. He chaffed Leeson in an explanatory letter, adding almost with a hint of envy: 'Commend me to the maid. You are a plutocrat. I have no maid: nor even a wife: whereas you have two women to look after you. Mohammedan!'

Letters poured from his pen throughout these last years, to literary friends or acquaintances such as E.M. Forster, Robert Graves, Frederic Manning, Noel Coward and Ezra Pound; frequently to Lady Astor; endlessly to Charlotte Shaw; to Trenchard, to the composer Sir Edward Elgar, but also to wartime colleagues such as Newcombe, or to friends from his early service days. He moved between a series of Air Force and marine establishments, visited Clouds Hill when he could (rejoicing in 1933 in the installation of a bath manufactured by his former ordnance officer at Akaba, Raymond Goslett, paid for out of the proceeds of his *Odyssey*), and as the work on speedboats prospered and showed significant results he even wrote an operational textbook.

In a letter to George, now Lord, Lloyd, formerly of his Cairo intelligence circle and ex-High Commissioner for Egypt, written in September 1934 – by which time the end of his period of service was all too rapidly approaching – he made the claim: 'My boat work for the R.A.F. (now extending to the Army and Navy) has been successful, and lets me out of the Service with some distinction,

Lawrence on one of his seven Brough motorcycles; photograph taken at R.A.F. Cranwell. Ironically in the light of future events, when writing to a former wartime comrade he referred to his machine as his 'safety-valve'.
Bodleian Library

I think. After having dabbled in revolt and politics it is rather nice to have been mechanically useful!' It rings almost like an epitaph, the subtext of which, perhaps, should be the significant fact that the air-sea rescue boats which emerged from this pioneer work would save numerous lives in the coming war.

Lawrence's final posting was to Bridlington, on the Yorkshire coast, from where in the winter of 1934–35 he contemplated an uncertain future. In a letter to his friend of Carchemish days, Mrs Fontana, he wrote: 'My February-looming discharge from the Air Force makes me low-toned. It is like a hermit-crab losing his twelve-years-old shell, and I hate the pleasure that my service has been, coming thus to an arbitrary end.'

As that end neared, newspaper harassment was again much on his mind. Thus he wrote to 'Robbie' Robertson, fully aware that when he became a civilian he would be deprived of Robertson's invaluable help as shield and defender: 'Damn the Press... and when I'm "out", one of my greatest losses will be that of my "Publicity Deflector".' Once again, as so often, Robertson was fielding a request from some would-be interviewer and seeking guidance from Lawrence as to how to respond. He answered:

'What line I wish you to take'! I wish, like Nero, that the Press had but one neck, and that you would squeeze it. I wish... what do I wish? I wish I were dead, I think. These endings of careers are hurtful things, and I haven't an idea beyond my discharge, and only 25/- [25 shillings] a week, and no courage to take another job, because these news-hounds would smell it out and bay about it. Damn them, as I said. The only way to avoid mention is to join their number, and I'd see them all boiled in paraffin wax first.

Robertson was clearly concerned about the future of his eccentric aircraftman following his return to civilian life and was anxious to keep in contact. Lawrence wrote: ' "Look in when I'm next in town?" Yes, if I can: but I have no plans, beyond that of lying doggo for a while... Alas and alas: why must good things end and one grow old? I don't want to grow old... ever.' There was even a kick at the press in his final sentence: 'Give the News Chronicle my detestations, whenever they call! Yours T E Shaw.'

'What line I wish you to take'! I wish, like Nero, that the Press had but one neck, and that you would squeeze it. I wish... what do I wish? I wish I were dead, I think.

On 25 February 1935 Lawrence left Bridlington and the R.A.F. and headed south, not on his Brough, which was unlicensed at the time, but on a bicycle. The bicycle had been his first means of transport; now, as he began what would be in effect his final journey, he was riding one again, if a distinctly more conventional model than the drop-handled speedster of his youth. He intended to visit the novelist Frederic Manning at Bourne in Lincolnshire but then heard news of Manning's death and rode on. He called on his brother Arnold, now a don at Cambridge, on John Buchan at Elsfield Manor near Oxford, and hearing that the press was besieging Clouds Hill lurked briefly in London taking lodgings under a new alias, Mr E. Smith, and firing off letters to explain his predicament. To an M.P. friend, Ernest Thurtle, whom Lawrence had supported in a campaign to abolish military executions, he wrote: 'I wander about London in a queer unrest, wondering if my mainspring will ever have a tension to it again.' He approached the Press Association and the Press Photographing Agencies with requests to be left alone, then made for Clouds Hill only to find that the hounds were hard on his heels. One visit by two over-persistent journalists, who threw stones at his roof to bring him out, ended in a fist fight, prompting his neighbour and aide Pat Knowles to recall later: 'I have never been in the presence of anyone before or since in whom I felt such distress, anger and frustration.'

At some point he was in London again, Robertson noting on the envelope in which he kept Lawrence's February letter: 'His last visit to me at the A.M. [Air Ministry] was on 19th March 1935.' On that same day Lawrence wrote to Winston Churchill seeking help in coping with the 'press people' – 'I'm sorry to appeal in this way, but they have got me properly on the run' – to which Churchill responded by inviting him to his home at Chartwell, in Kent. He bicycled there on the following Sunday, though all he could draw from the visit was sympathy and encouragement, Churchill himself being in the political wilderness at this time.

By April he was back in Dorset and – a development ever important for his morale – remounted on his motorcycle, his seventh and last, acquired in 1932. He wrote to its maker George Brough: 'It goes like a shell, and seems as good as new.' The push-bike had been 'dull hard work when the wind is against' but delightful in lanes and sheltered places. He foresaw a mixed economy using both, but it seems the Brough soon took precedence.

The letters of Lawrence's final weeks send contradictory signals. Earlier in the year he had had cards printed with the legend: 'To tell you that in future I shall write very few letters', yet wrote letters on the back when sending them. In one to Lady Astor refusing an invitation to visit Cliveden – not for social reasons but as part of a move among a number of influential people, who valued his political acumen and military experience, to draw him into the task of reorganising the country's defence forces – he answered firmly 'No: wild mares would not at present take me away from Clouds Hill.' He added: 'Also there is something broken in the works... my will, I think. In this mood I would not take on any job at all.' He had used the 'something wrong in the works' formula back in 1929, and another variant appeared at this time, repeated more than once. Thus he wrote on 6 May to Bruce Rogers: 'At present the feeling is mere bewilderment. I imagine leaves must feel like this after they have fallen from the tree and until they die.' A letter to Eric Kennington written the same day including the fallen leaf metaphor ended with what almost seemed like a valediction: 'Peace to everybody'. Yet other letters were more positive. To a former Tank Corps friend 'Posh' Palmer, who was in a mood of suicidal depression, he wrote inviting him to visit, assuring him that 'at Clouds Hill there are no gas ovens, so I shall look forward to seeing you this summer as soon as all the plants have been watered'. To an Ashmolean friend, Karl Parker, he wrote on 12 May: 'At present I'm sitting in my cottage and getting used to an empty life', yet added that he was looking forward to the time when 'that spell is over and I begin to go about again'. There were signs too that the old urge to make fine books was beginning to re-surface; he had even selected a frontispiece for a limited edition of *The Mint.*

On the following day Pat Knowles brought him his post among which was a letter from Henry Williamson proposing a visit to Clouds Hill. Lawrence took out his Brough, rode down to Bovington Post Office, and despatched a telegram: 'Lunch Tuesday wet fine cottage one mile north Bovington Camp SHAW'. Somewhere ahead of him as he made his way back, two errand boys were cycling in the direction of Clouds Hill. It was a fine May morning, windless enough for Pat Knowles to hear the shouts of the instructors drilling their recruits down at the camp. He could also hear the engine of the motorcycle on its return journey; and then he heard it cut out, and stop.

By a curious irony, the war hero who died to national and international grief on 19 May 1935, from a severe head trauma received when falling from his Brough after clipping the wheel of an errand boy's bicycle, has acquired a kind of afterlife as a notable medical case. He was attended during his fatal coma by an assistant surgeon to the London Hospital, Mr Hugh Cairns, Australian born, a Balliol College Rhodes Scholar, and Rockefeller Travelling Fellow to the United States, who was a rising star in the field of neurosurgery. Cairns drove a hundred miles from his home in Arundel, Sussex, to Bovington, where he was profoundly moved by the tragedy of this famously gifted man dying from what he saw as

Preparing the public for the death of a national hero. The press laid siege to the military hospital at Bovington during the six days in which Lawrence lay in a coma. Meanwhile his cottage at Clouds Hill was put under guard to deter thieves or souvenir hunters.
The Oxford Times, BL *Newspaper Library, Colindale*

"Lawrence Of Arabia": Grave Condition

CONCUSSION: FRACTURE OF SKULL FEARED

SMASH SCENE BARRED TO PUBLIC

The condition of "Lawrence of Arabia" (otherwise Mr. T. E. Shaw, until recently an aircraftman in the Royal Air Force), who is in Wool Military Hospital, Bovington, Dorset, following a road accident, was stated late this afternoon to be "fairly critical." He is still unconscious.

CAPT. KNIGHT, staff captain at Bovington Camp, earlier stated that Mr. Shaw was suffering from concussion and a fractured skull was feared. Anxiety for his condition is caused chiefly, it is understood, by what the effect of the shock of the accident may be.

It is stated that a London specialist has flown down to be in attendance on Lawrence.

The accident occurred about midday yesterday while Lawrence was returning, after a visit to the camp, to his home at Clouds Hill, about a mile to the north of the camp.

He was riding a powerful motor-cycle and was thrown heavily. After the accident he was picked up by the driver of a lorry and taken to the military hospital.

Albert Hargraves, aged 14 (employed by a Bovington firm of butchers, for whom he started work three weeks ago), with whom Mr. Shaw collided, is also in hospital, suffering from concussion.

LAWRENCE'S SUPREME EFFORT

Lawrence, it is understood, made a supreme effort to avert the collision and only just failed to do so.

" My boy is suffering from shock, but we cannot see him until Wednesday, and although we inquired at the hospital last night we were only told that he was comfortable," said Mrs. Hargraves to-day.

The accident occurred at Clouds Hill —part of the heath known to the military as "Hell Fire Corner."

To-day, no one was allowed near the scene of the accident, where a mounted member of the military police was on duty.

Police constables, villagers and even the wives of soldiers in the Royal Tank Corps are not being allowed to say anything regarding the accident.

The wife of a Royal Tank Corps private said that military orders issued yesterday contained a clause that no visitors were to be allowed in the hospital.

Col. Thomas Edward Lawrence, who changed his name to Shaw by deed poll in 1927, won the title of " Uncrowned King of Arabia " by his achievement in uniting the Arab tribes against the Turks during the War.

The valuable aid he rendered during the Palestine campaign was regarded as a decisive factor in the Eastern war.

Since the War his movements have always had an air of mystery. He joined the Royal Tank Corps as a private and later transferred to the Royal Air Force as a mechanic in the name of " A. C. Ross," but his identity was soon discovered.

While in the Air Force he consistently refused promotion and devoted his leisure time to writing.

He left the service in March this year, and lately has been preparing his cottage at Moreton for his return to civilian life.

Mr. Shaw is closely associated with Oxford. He was educated at Oxford High School under the late Mr. A. W. Cave, and at Jesus College and Magdalen, of which he was Senior Demy.

Lawrence of Arabia."

SNOW & HAIL IN OXFORD

HEAVY FALLS IN THE NORTH

IN many parts of the country wintry conditions are being experienced to-day. In East Oxford and Headington districts snow began to fall about noon, but it soon turned to hail, and later this spread to the City.

Snow fell in the early morning at Duns Tew and Sandford, near Banbury and from noon onwards Banbury was swept by driving showers of sleet.

The Campsie and Kilsyth Hills in Stirlingshire were to-day covered with snow. Such a late fall is exceedingly rare.

Wintry conditions also prevail in the Peak district of Derbyshire. Longstone Edge, near Bakewell, had a covering of snow this morning.

Snow fell, too, at Leicester. In some other parts of the country, including Birmingham and Market Rasen, Lincs, there were hail showers.

The hailstorms, together with bitterly cold weather, caused damage on the flower farms of Lincolnshire.

A cricket match between Derbyshire and Yorkshire at Chesterfield was held up by a heavy snowstorm.

JUBILEE DAY CONTRAST

Snow fell in Central London to-day and was followed by a heavy shower of sleet. It was cold enough for winter, the temperature at mid-day being 43 degrees.

London was bathed in sunshine for 11 hours on Jubilee Day, only eight days ago, when the average temperature was 77 degrees.

'WANTED TO BE PATRIOTIC'

A man who pleaded " Guilty " to stealing a Union Jack flag and pole from a butcher's shop on 5 May because he " wanted to be patriotic " was bound over for six months by the stipendiary magistrate (Lord Ilkeston) at Birmingham to-day.

REPRIEVE FOR MURDERESS

Home Office Decision on Mrs. De La Mare

LIFE SENTENCE

MRS. DE LA MARE, the 27-year old Guernsey housekeeper, sentenced to death on 16 April for the murder of her 76-year-old farmer-employer, Alfred Brouard, has been reprieved.

Her counsel, Mr. H. H. Randall, received notification to-day from the Home Secretary that the sentence had been commuted to one of imprisonment for life.

The Home Secretary's decision follows his consideration of a full report of the trial. There is no Court of Appeal in the Island.

Mrs. De La Mare was alleged to have cut Mr. Brouard's throat with a knife as he slept in his farm-house at Le Camp Colnet on 6 February.

JURATS' FINDINGS

At her trial, conducted with the ancient ceremonial of Channel Islands legal procedure, she was found " Guilty " by each of the 11 jurats.

By a majority of six votes to five they found her sane at the time she committed the crime. Insanity had been the defence plea.

Mrs. De La Mare was the first woman to be tried for murder in the Channel Islands.

Since her conviction Mrs. De La Mare has been spending most of her time sewing and writing in her cell in the island gaol at St. Peter Port.

She is the only woman prisoner in the gaol and has been looked after day and night in the condemned cell by a special staff of wardresses.

SCENE IN CELL

The Sheriff of the island, who had been responsible for the carrying out of the death-sentence, entered the cell, accompanied by the prison governor, and told Mrs. De La Mare of the official decision.

A member of her lawyer's staff said that Mrs De La Mare was overjoyed. " She wept with relief and thanked Providence that her life had been spared," he said. " She also expressed her heartfelt gratitude to Advocate Randell and Advocate Arnold for the successful culmination of their efforts on her behalf."

It is understood that Mrs. De La Mare will be transferred to a women's prison in this country, probably Aylesbury or Holloway.

The question of her mental condition, which was one of the issues at the trial, will, in due course, come up for official review now that a reprieve has been granted. It may be decided to transfer her to the women's section of Broadmoor.

IS TIPPING BRIBERY?

The question of whether tipping was bribery was discussed at the Rotary International Association at Margate to-day.

The President, Mr. Fred Gray, said that tipping was all a matter of intention. Some people tipped to get preferential treatment and others tipped in appreciation.

basically an unnecessary cause. Indeed, thanks to Cairns, Lawrence was to become a powerful argument for the use of crash helmets by motorcyclists, whose numerous deaths before their introduction has been tellingly described as a 'modern epidemic'. As in the case of his work on speedboats, not a few people around the world would arguably owe their longer lives to the man whose relatively brief life ended abruptly in Dorset in 1935 at the age of forty-six.

The circumstances of his death, inevitably, have inspired controversy. There are those who have thought him the victim of a political assassination. There were stories of a mysterious black car being seen in the vicinity, but who would wish to kill him, and to what advantage? There have been claims that he committed suicide, but that would be a curious act just after inviting someone to lunch, and a criminal one if he had deliberately involved innocent errand boys in the attempt; fortunately the boys emerged relatively unscathed (though one suffered briefly from concussion), suggesting Lawrence was trying to evade them, not hit them. Although he frequently enjoyed the exhilaration of speed, there is no suggestion that he was going particularly fast as he headed back towards Clouds Hill that morning. The simplest and most obvious explanation is a lapse of concentration on a stretch of road which he had travelled so many times that he knew it almost too well, its very familiarity producing a fatal moment of carelessness. Here I as biographer declare my hand. My own personal conjecture – arrived at on instinct over forty years ago when I first walked the vicinity of Clouds Hill – is that, in the fraction of a second between the stirrup and the ground, among the myriad thoughts that can flash through the mind in such circumstances was a sudden intuition that this might be the solution, the exit, the appropriate deliverance, and that therefore he made no great effort to save himself as he crashed headlong on to the road.

9

'Jock, I'm very weary of being stared
at and discussed and praised. What
can one do to be forgotten? After I'm
dead they'll rattle my bones about, in
their curiosity. Au revoir.'

The rattling of the bones

'Jock, I'm very weary of being stared at and discussed and praised. What can one do to be forgotten? After I'm dead they'll rattle my bones about, in their curiosity. Au revoir.' Thus Lawrence writing to his R.A.F. friend Jock Chambers in 1929 not long after his return from India.

They rattled them reverentially at first. Among the mourners attending his funeral, at the beautiful parish church at Moreton just across the heath from Clouds Hill, were Mr and Mrs Winston Churchill, Lady Astor, Lord Lloyd, General Wavell, Augustus John and Siegfried Sassoon. The pall-bearers included Sir Ronald Storrs, Eric Kennington, Colonel Newcombe and Pat Knowles. His mother and elder brother were not present, being away, as they had been for some years, engaged in missionary work in China. However, Sarah Lawrence later chose the words for his headstone, the only description she allowed her son being 'Fellow of All Souls College Oxford' – there was no mention of his military or literary achievements – while the remaining space was devoted to a text from the Gospel of St John, Chapter 5: 'The hour is coming & now is when the dead shall hear the voice of the Son of God and they that hear shall live.' This would not have seemed suitable to Lawrence, but it clearly appealed to the woman whose long search for salvation dated back to the events at South Hill House in distant Ireland half a century earlier. It was as though she was claiming her distinctly sceptical son for her brand of faith, even in the grave.

Shortly a bust by Kennington appeared in St Paul's Cathedral, while a copy was placed in Jesus College outside the chapel; the copy of a fine portrait of him in Arab robes by Augustus John would later hang in the hall there, the original housed in the Tate Gallery in London. Meanwhile Kennington worked at the striking recumbent sculpture, again depicting him in Arab robes, hand clasped on dagger, that would find a permanent home in St Martin's Church, Wareham, Dorset.

From the creators of "The Bridge On The River Kwai."
Columbia Pictures presents The SAM SPIEGEL · DAVID LEAN Production of

LAWRENCE OF ARABIA

*"I deem him one of the greatest beings alive in our time.
...we shall never see his like again. His name will live in history.
It will live in the annals of war...It will live in the legends of Arabia!"*
—WINSTON CHURCHILL

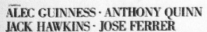

ALEC GUINNESS · ANTHONY QUINN
JACK HAWKINS · JOSE FERRER
ANTHONY QUAYLE · CLAUDE RAINS · ARTHUR KENNEDY
PETER O'TOOLE as LAWRENCE · OMAR SHARIF as "Ali"
ROBERT BOLT · SAM SPIEGEL · DAVID LEAN · TECHNICOLOR®

SUPER PANAVISION 70®

Seven Pillars of Wisdom, the public version of the subscribers' edition, came
out in the year of his death and sold in tens of thousands. The year 1937 saw the
publication of a book of tributes, eighty of them, edited by his brother Arnold
and entitled *T.E. Lawrence by his Friends*; while David Garnett produced a volume
of almost six hundred of his letters in 1938.

The 1939–45 war concentrated minds elsewhere, so that it was not until the
early 1950s that there was a significant revival of interest in him. The occasion was
the publication of a series of fine anthologies of well-known writers, of which
the one with possibly the greatest impact, appearing in 1951, was *The Essential*

T.E. Lawrence. Reviewers fell on it as on manna, praising it for the fact that it contained the first published extracts from *The Mint*, but above all for reminding readers that, at a time when yarns about resistance heroes or guerrilla groups operating deep in enemy territory were pouring from the presses, Lawrence had been there before all of them. Thus the anonymous reviewer in *The Times Literary*

Opposite: St Martin's Church, Wareham,
Dorset, home of the famous effigy of
Lawrence by Eric Kennington.
Rector of St Martin's Church, Wareham

Supplement, claiming the present moment as 'a particularly propitious
one for a new selection of [his] writings', enthused:

*In the past five years we have had numerous opportunities of studying the
exploits of a 'Popski' in the Western Desert, an Orde Wingate in Palestine and
Burma, of commandos and frogmen and paratroopers whose very existence to
the men of 1914–18, trapped in the miry insatiable inferno of the Somme,
would have seemed an overwrought fancy, the figment of some super-Wellsian
romance... [W]herever they operated – those small bands of happy fanatics who,
with knives in teeth and blackened faces, scaled enemy-held coastlines, swam
beneath rivers or dropped from the innocent clouds – all shared in their lesser
or greater degree the mantle of T. E. Lawrence...*

Similarly the distinguished writer and critic V. S. Pritchett, in an
eloquent review in the *New Statesman*, hailed him as 'a new and
prophetic prototype', in that 'in everything, from the hold-ups, the
executions, the intrigue and the tortures to the final nihilism, he was
the first guinea-pig of the underground.' Of *Seven Pillars* he wrote,
admiringly: 'Throughout a swift, masterly narrative, packed with action,
character and personal emotion, we have the extraordinary spectacle
of a brain working the whole time. It is as if we could see the campaign
thought by thought. The close texture of genius in action has never
been so livingly done by an active man...'

In 1955 the blow fell. Richard Aldington's debunking 'biographical
enquiry' (whose message was evident from the title of its French version,
published before the British edition as *Lawrence l'Imposteur*) attacked
Lawrence as a fraud and a failure, and publicised the fact of his

illegitimacy. This understandably caused distress to his mother, who would stoically bear the barbs while tenaciously retaining her belief in her exceptional son until her death in 1959 aged ninety-eight. A task force of his friends, disparagingly dubbed the 'Lawrence Bureau', gathered to his defence, but ever since then there has been open warfare, with a whole spectrum of biographers, from virtual worshippers to outright denigrators seeking to delineate and define him, deify or destroy him. As well as his family background his sexuality has been ruthlessly examined, with claim and counter-claim as to whether he was an active or non-active homosexual, a serial masochist obsessed by self-humiliation, or a victim wrestling with the disturbing consequences of abuse. His war record too was challenged, until, as he himself had foreseen, the emergence into the public domain of the documents of the time substantiated his accounts to a remarkable degree.

The year 1962 saw the casting of a powerful, different light on the matter of his reputation, with the release of a feature film about his exploits that was to become one of the most popular movies ever made. David Lean's *Lawrence of Arabia*, with Peter O'Toole in the title role, would become a classic, exporting an awareness of its central figure to the world's four corners and winning, despite some dissenting voices, a new generation of adherents. If nothing else, Lawrence would surely have approved of one particular achievement, that the film captured something of the profound and haunting beauty of the landscapes that had moved and captivated him half a century before.

Significantly, during all this, Lawrence the human being as opposed to Lawrence the hero was, importantly and necessarily, re-identified. Thus in a striking review in 1963 of the American paperback of *The Essential T.E. Lawrence*, the American critic Irving Howe welcomed a more contemporary Lawrence than the camel-mounted icon of earlier years:

Lawrence is not yet a name to be put away in history, a footnote in dust… His wartime record was remarkable, the basis of all that was to come; without it he might have been just another young man afflicted with post-war malaise. But what finally draws one to Lawrence, making him seem not merely an exceptional figure, but a representative man of our century, is his courage and vulnerability in bearing the burden of consciousness. 'One used to think that such frames of mind would have perished with the age of religion: and yet here they rise up, purely secular.'

The last sentence is from Lawrence himself, from one of his letters to Lionel Curtis written at Bovington in 1923.

It is this Lawrence, almost a kind of lay saint, if a deeply flawed one, who knew the real desert and also the desert of the mind, who despite all the flak or the fanfares continues to attract people around the world to read his works and visit his shrines. Speaking in his mid-eighties not many years before his death at the age of ninety-one, his brother A.W. Lawrence – the last of the line, Bob having died twenty years earlier aged eighty-six – stated in a moving deposition:

He seems to answer some sort of requirement. It's almost religious – in fact it is a religion. I had great difficulty in not allowing myself to be used as the St Paul of it. I had, I should think, something like five hundred letters after his death; the majority wanted me to take up his mantle. I suppose it was because of his disdain for worldly success. He wanted it when he was young; he got it; and despised it…

This might seem an appropriate last word on this extraordinary man, except that there can never be a last word, in that even as this present interpretation is being completed almost certainly somewhere else another is being planned. The quest goes on.